Just Not Today

Sydney M. Hunt

JUST NOT TODAY

"This book is dedicated to all law enforcement families. Your love, strength, and loyalty are what give us the courage to carry on. Thank you." –Officer Joe Garrett & Officer Marty Dulworth

Born to die… just not today.

Just Not Today

Foreword

I met Officer Marty Dulworth at a K9 conference in San Francisco in August 2017. I remember reading the brief description of his class, and I knew right away it was one I wanted to sit in on. I sat down and mentally prepared myself because I knew it was going to be an emotional few hours. Marty introduced himself, and I immediately noticed that we had a lot of similarities. We were the same age, similar years on with our departments, both K9 handlers, and we both had lost our K9 partners (my partner died of cancer at 5 years old). His presentation was about the night of July 26, 2012; the night when his whole world changed.

Marty described the night in great detail using raw emotion; he wasn't afraid to shed a tear. Marty described how he was shot, how he almost died, and how his brother and fellow officer, Joe Garrett, saved his life. He cried when he talked about losing Kilo, and I couldn't help but put myself in his shoes. I sat there trying to understand how difficult that night must have been.

There were several times where Marty spoke about his family, how much he loved them and how he wasn't going to quit for them. Hearing him talk about his young children, fiancé, his parents and the possibility of him dying broke my heart and had me bawling for a man that I had yet to meet. I again put myself in his shoes and thought about leaving behind the ones I loved for a job that I always wanted to do.

After the debrief was over, there was a standing ovation for Marty; many people were still in tears and disbelief. So many of us believed that we had just heard one of the greatest stories of survival ever in law enforcement. Many, if not all of us, had sat through a story of an officer being shot and surviving, but not one of those can compare to this story.

Marty showed a strength that few people have. He overcame a shooting that would have left most people physically and mentally defeated and unable to return to police work. Many officers in his situation would be unable and unwilling to overcome all of the obstacles that he had to overcome. But Marty knew that he was going to return to his job as a K9 handler.

After the debrief was over, I went up and shook Marty's hand, introduced myself, and let him know how much his story hit me emotionally and mentally. We quickly learned that we had colleagues in common, which was a surprise. It was from that handshake forward that Marty and I became friends, or what I now tell him: "the sister he never wanted".

I asked Marty if he would drive up to Buffalo Grove, Illinois and speak to officers in the Chicagoland area because I felt his story needed to be shared. Without hesitation, Marty agreed and the planning started immediately. Marty and I stayed in contact and, in early November, Marty and Joe came to Buffalo Grove and spoke to about 150 officers from Illinois and Wisconsin. Marty and Joe have since shared their story in Buffalo Grove seven different times and have reached several hundred officers, social workers, dispatchers, and civilians in the process. I have also traveled to various events with them to help share their story because I am so passionate about it.

I've made it a habit to tell their story to any officer that cares to listen. I have received such positive feedback from those who have chosen to attend the debrief session or listen to the podcast. They have all agreed that this a story that is second to none, and it truly shows the strength in Marty and Joe. It shows how, miraculously, everything that needed to go right, went right that evening. Marty, Joe and their extended families have become family to me. Their story has brought us together even though I wasn't there that night and even though we live 300 miles apart.

Hearing Marty's debrief that day in August had such a profound effect on me, that I left San Francisco and told Marty I would be "flipping a switch" and changing my life from that point forward. I immediately returned to Illinois, and started working out again. I am now physically and mentally in the best shape of my life. Prior to meeting Marty and Joe, I was going through the daily motions of being a veteran officer, and I was thankful for the safe community that I worked in. I have since learned to embrace The Warrior Mindset, and I constantly remind myself that at any time I could be in the same situation as Marty: lying on the ground and fighting for my life. I go to work each day, and I tell myself, "TODAY IS NOT THE DAY!"

K9 Officer Danielle Baron
Buffalo Grove Police Department
Buffalo Grove, IL

Part 1: Shots in the Dark

Chapter 1

When you think of badass police officer stories, you probably think of big cities, am I right? You think of the west side of Chicago, of tennis shoes hanging over electric lines, of dark alleys covered in graffiti. You think of flickering street lights that are struggling to hang on after years of illuminating grotesque, heart-wrenching scenes of bloodshed and loss. You think of putrid puddles next to overflowing dumpsters and rusty fire escapes. And, of course, you think of the police officers in their pristine uniforms executing clear-cut defense tactics while they return fire at the hellish gangsters who dare to disrupt the law and order of the city.

Now, let me tell you what you *don't* think of, and you'll forgive me if I sound smug, but I know I'm correct in this. You don't think of a forgotten town surrounded by miles and miles of cornfields, a town where people aren't afraid to leave their windows open at night and their vehicles unlocked. You don't think of a police officer wearing a tie-dyed t-shirt and jean shorts driving his truck through people's yards. And you *certainly* don't think of that police officer's trash man putting himself in harm's way to help a fallen officer.

Sadly, there are a lot of important things that people don't think of when they think of badass police officer stories. They don't think of what it feels like to be constantly aware of one's own mortality. They don't think of the coping mechanisms that their families have to use to deal with the fact that any "have a good shift" could be the last. They don't think of the physical and psychological turmoil after an officer is wounded, or after a department loses one of its own. Maybe you do think about this, reader, but you are likely either a police officer, related to a police officer, or you are simply in the minority.

There are thousands of amazing police officer stories out there, but I doubt you've ever heard one quite like this. So, buckle up and enjoy the ride. It's going to be a bumpy one.

Our story begins on July 26th, 2012 in the flyover state of Indiana. There are many words one could use to describe an Indiana summer, but the two most accurate words? Humid and hot. And not the kind of humidity that just makes your hair frizz, but the kind of humidity that makes you feel like you hopped out of the shower and put your clothes on without bothering to dry yourself off first.

It was one of those kinds of days when Officer Marty Dulworth was working on his pole barn in the small and oft-forgotten town of Middletown, Indiana. He worked for the Anderson Police Department to the west, but Middletown offered a haven of tranquility away from the noise and chaos of the city. His entire family lived in the town, as well, so it really was a place of peace and happiness.

It was just after 7:30 in the morning when his fianceé Jessica walked out of the house to check on him.

"How's it coming along?" she asked.

"Good," he replied.

"Good. Ryan's staying tonight, but Hayley's going to stay with her mom."

Ryan and Hayley were his two children from his previous marriage, but Jess loved them as her own.

"I think I might use some vacation time and stay home tonight, then. Spend some time with you and Ryan, get an early start on this tomorrow morning."

Marty worked third shift at the police department, the craziest and toughest shift to work. It wasn't just tough on Marty, though; it was tough on Jess, too. It's easier to not worry about your police officer fiancé when you both work during the day, but when he works at night and you're expected to just go to sleep? That's when things get tricky.

"You need to save your vacation time for after the wedding," Jess replied as she turned to head back into the house. "Just go in tonight; the pole barn will still be here. Plenty of time to get it done."

He decided it was best not to argue, so he conceded and continued working. He would need his time off for the days before and after the wedding. Before the wedding, there was much to get done, and after the wedding, well, he wanted to soak in as much time with his new wife as possible without having to worry about the criminals and general chaos of Anderson.

He smiled as he took a short break from his work. He couldn't believe that in just two short weeks, he would be marrying the woman of his dreams. Life had been a struggle before he met Jess, and though things weren't perfect now, they were a million times better with her around.

He had a job he loved, a family who had his back, and a beautiful woman he would soon be able to call his wife. Life was good.

6

"Hey Marty!"

Marty was so caught up in his thoughts that he had completely ignored the sound of the trash truck pulling up in front of his house.

"Hey Larry!" he said as he waved to his trash collector and headed toward him. "How's it going?"

Larry was a large man, and he would have seemed intimidating to some if it weren't for the enormous smile that was almost always plastered on his face.

"Good. How are you?"

"Good, thanks," Marty replied as he wiped the sweat from his brow.

Though their conversations were always short, Marty was quite fond of Larry. He was a pleasant guy who only ever had kind words to say. He was an avid police-scanner listener, and he enjoyed going over the previous night's events with Marty.

Those were always their conversations. The usual "how are you" bit and gossiping about the criminals of Anderson. However, every now and then, another topic of conversation would arise, a question would be asked: "Marty, when ya takin' me on a ride-along?"

And always, the time just wasn't right, or it would just be too boring, or some other excuse. It wasn't that Marty didn't like Larry; he did. It was just that Marty enjoyed his routine.

And on top of all that, ride-alongs were stressful. Marty always felt like he had to entertain his ride-along, like he had to make it seem as though being a police officer were glamorous or like the movies.

It wasn't.

It wasn't at all.

On this morning, though, Larry didn't ask to ride-along with him. It had been a while since he had asked, Marty thought. As he watched his trash collector prepare to move along, something in him made him call out to stop him. Something told him that that day was a good day.

"Hey Larry, you got plans tonight?" Marty asked before the truck drove away.

"Nope. Not a thing," Larry replied.

"Wanna go on a ride-along?"

An enormous smile emerged on Larry's face, and something in his eyes seemed to shout: "I can't believe it!"

"Absolutely!" he replied. "That'd be awesome!"

"Alright," Marty replied with a chuckle. "Don't get too excited. It probably won't be as cool as you think. I'll pick you up at the Ricker's on Scatterfield and 53rd between 9:30 and 10."

Larry thanked him and moved along down the road. From the look on his face, Marty was entirely convinced that Larry didn't believe him when he said it wouldn't be exciting.

Marty didn't really understand why he had offered to take him on a ride-along that night. Perhaps it was because he felt like the luckiest man in the world, and this feeling of happiness and good fortune just demanded to be shared. Or perhaps it was a reason much deeper than that, a reason that he couldn't possibly understand at that time. Perhaps it was Providence pulling the strings, and knowing that Larry was a character that needed to be added to this story.

As is common in one's daily life, however, Marty did not think on his own reasoning too much, but instead focused on what was in front of him. There was work to be done, after all. He did, however, allow himself to daydream just a little bit about the beautiful present and the even more beautiful future that would soon be his.

.

.

Chapter 2

The heat of the day was starting to fade away, and a cool evening breeze refreshed the city as Marty walked to his car after roll call. Marty had told Larry that he would pick him up at the gas station between 9:30 and 10:00, but he knew that that wasn't going to happen from the moment he pulled out of the station parking lot; the night was off to a busy start. He texted his trash man a heads-up:

Might be a little late.

At 10:40, he pulled up to the gas station and saw Larry standing on the curb in a T-shirt and jeans holding two 44oz pops.

"Sorry I'm late," Marty said. "Had a situation to take care of. Hop in."

Larry hopped in the passenger seat and assured Marty that he understood his tardiness. He handed Marty his pop, and he sipped on his as he stared at the officer with eager eyes. The excitement wasn't just evident in his eyes, though. His smile was enormous, and every inch of him seemed alert, focused and ready for anything.

As Marty looked at his trash man, he couldn't help but feel that he would be disappointed at the end of the ride-along. However, he figured that just getting the chance to be in a police car (in the passenger seat, anyway) would be a grand adventure to a man who had only ever heard about the police nightlife over a scanner. Marty couldn't help but return the smile for a split second, but he quickly put his serious face on to lay down the ground rules.

Well, technically there was really only one rule.

"If things go south, at NO time do you get out of this vehicle unless it's on fire," Marty commanded. "Got it?"

"Got it!" Larry replied.

"Good," Marty said. "Okay, so here's the plan."

Larry was as attentive as a school child in the front row of class. He was sitting up straight, his eyes locked onto Marty's.

"We'll drive around a bit and see what happens. I'll drop you back off here in a few hours, or sooner if you get bored. That's pretty much it. That's the plan. That's all I've got."

Larry nodded his head and took a few more sips of his pop as Marty pulled out of the gas station and began heading west on 53rd St. The two men maintained a surface level conversation as the police car rolled onward toward nowhere in particular.

There is one important character in this story that hasn't been mentioned yet that was sitting ever so quietly, ever so attentively throughout their conversation. He was sitting in the back seat, listening but saying nothing. He was 85 pounds of pure beast, and equal parts, if not more, of loyalty.

You see, Marty Dulworth wasn't just an ordinary police officer; he was a part of the K9 Unit. And the quiet character in the back seat? His fearsome, intelligent, and, of course, handsome partner: Kilo, a Belgian Malinois.

Kilo and Marty were more than just partners, more than just friends; Kilo had, in more ways than one, saved Marty's life. Marty had joined the Anderson Police Department in 2001, but it wasn't until 2008 that he joined the K9 Unit. Marty's first dog, Fedor, another Belgian Malinois, was a police canine through and through. He was well-behaved, determined, and all-around a handler's dream. In June of 2009, however, something happened that would change Marty's path forever.

The years leading up to 2009 had been a struggle. His marriage over, his relationship with his two children on the fringe, and alcohol becoming his closest friend; Marty was in over his head. If one were to tell someone that being a police officer is a stressful job, it is unlikely that you would receive disagreement. But, do people really understand *how* stressful? Do people really understand what that kind of stress does to a person's mind? Philosophers and poets throughout the ages have said that there is no escaping one's own mind, but humans will always seek out ways to try.

Partying night after night. Sleeping with woman after woman. Drink after drink after drink. He was spiraling; he knew that he was. But it was easier to spiral than it was to face the demons that were pulling him down.

The bad thing about spiraling, though, is that you can't spiral forever. You either find a way to pull yourself back up, or you hit rock bottom.

On June 6th, 2009, on his way home from a party, Officer Marty Dulworth was pulled over, arrested, and charged with a DUI.

It was one of the darkest times in his life. His work, though it was a source of incredible stress, was also what he took pride in, what he loved doing. At the end of the day, that was who he was. He was a police officer, and he couldn't imagine being anything else. But as he was faced with the charges against him, he had to consider that that might be his fate.

He was given a 62-day suspension. No pay. Two months of unwanted freedom gave him plenty of time to reconsider many things in his life. In the present looking back, he thinks it possible that the DUI would have been enough to set him back on the right path, but he also knows that it would not have been as enjoyable a journey without Kilo.

Kilo started out as a *very* badly-behaved dog. And what better partner for a post-suspension police officer than a badly behaved dog? The head of the K9 Unit deemed that Kilo would be Marty's project. Or, perhaps, Marty would be Kilo's project. Regardless of how you look at it, the two of them would draw one another out of their separate dark places.

From having to feed Kilo through a locked kennel to preserve his own limbs, to accepting their trophy at the K9 Olympics in Peru, Indiana in 2010, the two climbed to the top and stayed there.

Kilo was a family dog, too. Jess and the kids loved their ever-watchful protector, and even Marty's parents and extended family couldn't help but adore him.

"Officer shot in Pendleton"

The words over the radio yanked Marty away from his reminiscing. He looked over to Larry who had a look on his face that said, "What did they just say?!"

Marty listened for the location: near East and John.

Pendleton wasn't his territory, really, but it didn't matter. An officer was in trouble. Civilians were in trouble. There was no time to lose. He grabbed the radio.

"K9-4 en route."

Chapter 3

Pendleton was a small city to the south of Anderson. It was known for its charming downtown, its beautiful Falls Park, and its festivals in the fall. It wasn't unusual for APD to help out their neighbor; the Pendleton Police Department was very small. However, Marty really didn't know his way around the town, so he pulled over when he saw two police officers parked along the side of the road.

"Hey guys," Marty said as he approached them. "Is this where the shots were fired?"

The police officer informed him that, no, the shots were fired at the corner of East and John a few blocks over. Marty wondered why they were parked there, then, and not at the site, but he decided that it didn't matter in the moment. He hopped back in the car and headed down the street.

Marty and Larry arrived at the scene at the same time as three other APD officers. Out of one car stepped Officer Gabe Bailey, another K9 officer (K9-3). Out of another stepped Officer Matt Guthrie, and out of the third stepped Officer Shaun Williams. One thing that all police officers will attest to is that the best thing you can have in a bad situation is great backup.

Marty hopped out of the car and immediately got Kilo from the back seat. Though he thought he may not end up needing Kilo, he lived by the following philosophy: "I'd rather have my partner and not need him than need him and not have him."

After he got Kilo out, Marty saw two people down the street a little ways. Civilians who apparently were interested in what was going on. Marty shook his head.

"Have you two heard any gunshots?" Marty shouted at them.

They nodded their heads and pointed down a dark alley. Marty stared down the alley and immediately thought, "Are you kidding me?"

Marty had served in the United States Marine Corps for four years, and he had been a police officer for eleven. He had been in numerous dangerous situations, dealing with violent criminals and foreign enemies. These situations were ones that would steal the color from the faces of average people, but it was normal for Marty. However, there was one thing that was able to strike fear into the core of his being, one enemy that, although he faced it frequently, was still his most dreaded foe.

Marty was terrified of the dark.

And, of course, this shooter decides that the best place to shoot at people was in a dark alley at night with only the light of the stars to illuminate his way. Marty stared down the alley and accepted the inevitable: he was going to have to face the darkness.

It is almost comical, really, to think that a police officer could be more afraid of the dark than of an active shooter. But, when you think about it, it makes sense in some ways. Because, you see, darkness isn't just the absence of light. It's much more than that.

Darkness is uncertainty.

Darkness is vulnerability.

Darkness is an evening out of the playing field between you and your enemy.

Marty's fear of darkness began much earlier in his life, however, long before he joined the Marine Corps. Marty had always loved the light and despised the dark, and there was one person who knew this better than any other: his older brother, Joe.

Joe was seventeen years Marty's senior. You would think that this significant age difference would have made their relationship a nurturing one, one where Joe took care of Marty and encouraged him due to his impressionability. It was, however, quite the opposite. Because, you see, few things brought Joe more joy than terrorizing his little brother.

Joe could be quite creative with his terror. When he was home from the Marine Corps when Marty was just eight years old, he called his elementary school to tell the office he needed to pick his little brother up early. When he collected his brother, he informed him that both their parents had died in a car accident. It wasn't until their parents got home from work that Marty realized his brother had lied to him. And though the story is one that makes Joe look like a sinister sociopath, it is his favorite story to tell.

Joe wasn't always as creative as he was in that instance, though he was always resourceful. He knew what Marty was afraid of, and he knew how to use that to his advantage. Marty couldn't count the number of times that Joe had jumped out of dark places and nearly scared him to death. These instances, combined with the uncertainty and vulnerability that came with darkness, were enough to make Marty *always* carry two flashlights, and more than enough to make him stare down that dark alley on that summer night and think: "Well, shit."

"You two should get inside," Marty hollered back at the two civilians. "It's not safe out here."

The two people did as they were told, and Marty walked toward his fellow officers.

"Well, what's the plan?" Bailey asked.

"Civilians say that shots were fired down the alley," Marty replied as he pointed him in the right direction.

They wasted no time. The four Anderson officers and Kilo started toward the dark alley, but they didn't get very far before a woman called to them from her front door. She lived in one of the houses on the corner.

"My garage door is open!" she shouted as she pointed to the end of the dark alley. "It's never open! I think someone is in there!"

Marty let out a sigh of relief.

"Perfect," he thought. "We can just go through her yard and around to the back. No dark alley tonight!"

"Go back inside, ma'm," Williams called out. "Is it okay if we cut through your yard?"

"Oh, that gate is broken," she replied. "You'd have to hop the fence."

Shit.

Williams looked to Marty who shrugged his shoulders.

"Down the alley it is, then," Marty said.

They took it slowly and carefully. They got further down the alley, and things looked okay. They saw nothing, no one. When they got about twenty-five feet down the alley, however, was when it happened, and it all happened so fast.

It felt like somebody took a baseball bat and knocked Marty's feet out from under him. He lay on the ground staring up at the sky, knowing something was wrong but not being able to get his brain to process what was happening. It was as if the stars themselves had hypnotized him. While the stars overwhelmed his vision, gunpowder overwhelmed his sense of taste.

But, still, he couldn't bring himself to move. Time seemed to stand still as he continued staring at the stars, his only source of light.

It wasn't long, however, before another source of light appeared, a more sinister one. To his left, he saw a dark silhouette coming toward him from the other end of the alley, a dark silhouette that carried a rifle with fire coming out of the end of it.

One round after another.

One round after another.

And it was then that the pieces finally came together. He stared at this figure coming toward him and thought, "Uh, okay, I think I've been shot."

What felt like several minutes to Marty was only seconds to everyone else, including Kilo. Marty's ever-loyal partner wasted no time coming to his rescue. He jumped on top of Marty and started barking at the figure. For a split second, Marty thought that Kilo's voice sounded a little funny, but his brain didn't allow him to dwell on the thought. After all, there was a crazy person shooting at him.

All he could think was that he had to get up if he was going to survive. However, when he looked down at his feet, he realized that his left foot was facing the wrong way. Clearly, the shot had done more damage than he had thought. So, standing wasn't an option. Crawling it was, then.

He crawled backwards as fast as he could, but the dark figure moved faster.

Round after round.

Round after round.

Suddenly, there was an excruciating pain in his right leg, and all he could think was, "This guy is going to shoot me up right here in this dark alley. This is it."

It was in that moment of despair, however, that Officer Matt Guthrie raised his AR and began returning fire. This was brilliant news for Marty; he had a chance to try to put some space between him and this shooter. However, it wasn't such great news for Officer Shaun Williams. Williams reached down to try to help Marty to safety, but Kilo saw a more sinister plot unfolding.

An important thing to remember about police canines, reader, is that they are fiercely loyal. However, their loyalty is not to all cops; their loyalty is to their handler and *only* to their handler. They are trained to see danger in every situation, and they react accordingly.

Let's review the situation. The alley is dark. Kilo's handler has been shot by an unfamiliar figure. An officer is returning fire. And now a strange man unfamiliar to Kilo is reaching for his handler, his partner. Williams didn't stand a chance.

As soon as Williams grabbed Marty, Kilo attacked. And when Kilo attacked someone, it wasn't one bite and done. He bit him over and over again, and an already chaotic situation became even more chaotic.

In between Williams' cries of pain, Marty yelled at Kilo to return to him. He tried over and over again, but he wouldn't listen. He had always listened before. Always.

Part of being a police officer means making difficult calls. Marty was used to this burden from serving in the Marine Corps, but it didn't make it easier. Nothing could have helped in this moment.

He didn't have time to think about all the ways that Kilo had helped him, how Kilo had saved him. He didn't have time to remember their first days together when Kilo wanted to tear Marty apart limb by limb while Marty fed him through the kennel gate. He didn't have time to reminisce on their K9 Olympics victory. There was no time.

He had to make a decision, and he had to do it in a matter of seconds.
It was the most difficult decision he had ever made in his entire life.

"Guthrie!" he yelled. "Shoot the dog!"

Guthrie stopped firing into the darkness and turned to Marty with a look of surprise.

"You have to shoot the dog!" Marty yelled. "Shoot him!"

Guthrie turned toward Kilo and took the shot. And as the lifeless body of Marty's partner lay beside him, he had no time to mourn.

They were still in danger. They were still in darkness.

They needed to find cover, and they needed to find it quick.

Chapter 4

Officer Joe Garrett enjoyed his part-time job working security for the psych rooms at St. Vincent Anderson Regional Emergency Department, he really did. You might not think so, though, if you were to observe him in this habitat. He walked in the building with a straight face, and he sat in the security room with a straight face, and he even held conversations with a straight face, no matter the topic. But, he also *left* the hospital after his shift with a straight face, so he was always consistent. And he never called in. So, the general consensus was that, despite the straight face, he enjoyed his job.

A majority of evenings at the hospital were devoid of excitement for Joe. Most of the psych patients were surprisingly cooperative, and the difficult ones became cooperative once they were dosed with Geodon. There was the occasional jail clearance patient who caused problems and made Joe hop up out of his seat but, for the most part, it was an okay gig.

On the night of July 26th, 2012, Joe walked out of the emergency room with his typical straight face. The evening had been a slow one, thankfully, but he was still more than ready to get home and get some rest. As he got closer to his truck, he thought to reach and turn his radio off; that was his habit. He hated listening to the police radio when he wasn't on the clock. His philosophy was: "I've been at this for long enough. Let the rookies have all the fun."

He quickly realized, however, that turning off the radio would come at the cost of the fountain pop he was holding. He figured he would turn it off when he got into the truck, but the thought escaped him as he buckled his seatbelt and pulled out of the parking lot. There was no radio traffic at that moment, though, so turning it off wasn't a priority.

It was Joe's habit to stop by the police station and change out of his uniform there rather than at his home. He was a private man, a man who enjoyed his routine and spending time alone. He had a wife and four children at home. He lived within a quarter-mile radius of his parents, his brother Mark, and his brother Marty. He enjoyed being around his family, of course; he loved them. But he just couldn't help the fact that he thrived on these moments of solitude.

When he reached the police station, he had pretty much lost interest in turning the radio off. He was more focused on getting inside and getting into a comfier set of clothes. As soon as he began to step out of the truck, however, he heard a concerning call come over the radio: a police officer in Pendleton had been shot.

It was disheartening, of course, to hear that a fellow officer had been shot. Joe wasn't on the clock, though, and it had been an incredibly long day.

He decided, however, that he would go to the scene and be an extra set of eyes, a warm body they could use if need be. But, he was still going to change out of his uniform; that much was decided.

He went into the locker room and changed into his preferred outfit: a pair of denim shorts that were far too big for him, a tie-dyed t-shirt, and his "Jesus sandals".

If I had to guess, reader, I would assume you're probably thinking that this absurd of an outfit on this serious of a man is comical at the most and interesting at the least. If you really knew Joe Garrett, however, it would seem to you to be the most fitting outfit imaginable.

Beneath his serious and sometimes melancholic exterior was the most sarcastic, driest sense of humor that exists on God's Green Earth. He enjoyed nothing more than saying things that took people back, that made their eyes grow large, and that, subsequently, made them at best let out a hearty laugh and at worst think, "Is this guy psychologically unstable?" His ensemble would certainly make people do one of those two things, and nothing less could be expected of Officer Joe Garrett.

He returned to his truck and hopped onto MLKJ Blvd, the road that would take him into Pendleton. He didn't know exactly where the scene was, but he knew the general vicinity, and the multitude of police vehicles would be difficult to miss.

If there's one thing that has been made clear about Joe Garrett already, it's that he is not an easily excitable person. Was he concerned and upset that a police officer had been shot? Naturally. Was the adrenaline rushing through his veins? Was his heart rate through the roof? No. He was cool and collected. This unexcitable nature, however, didn't develop over night.

Joe had served in the Marine Corps long before his little brother. 28 and a half years he spent between in the military putting himself in danger all over the world, and it was this experience that gave him his Warrior Mindset.

"What is the Warrior Mindset?", you ask.

A warrior does not allow fear to overtake him.

A warrior focuses on the mission.

A warrior prepares for the worst, yet remains firm in his belief that he will overcome the worst, should it occur.

This is the Warrior Mindset. This was Joe Garrett's mindset on this day and every day.

The Warrior Mindset was a part of his DNA, so much so that not even what he heard over the radio could make him stray from it.

"K9-4. I have been shot!"

It took Joe only a moment to realize what he *thought* he heard, but he had to be sure. He grabbed his radio.

"Unit 207," he began. "Did he say K9-4?"

"Affirmative," replied dispatch.

The mission had changed now; it had changed drastically. It wasn't just a police brother in danger now; it was his blood brother. It was his little brother.

"I'm enroute to Pendleton," Joe said into the radio.

He immediately laid on the accelerator. Before long, he came up on a police car heading to the scene: a perfect way for Joe to get where he needed to go. The speedometer read 115 as he tailed the car so closely that he couldn't see the license plate. He and the car in front of him blazed right through the perimeter set up by EMA.

Focus on the mission.

Focus on the mission.

He kept following the car, but soon he realized that the lights and chaos were now behind him. They had missed the turn needed to take them to the scene.

Well, focus on the mission, right?

Joe made a sharp left turn and drove straight into a field. There was no time for turning around or going around; he went through. Through anything and everything in his path. The bumps had his bottom flying up out of the seat.

The first thing to go was the exhaust, and the "Check Engine" light illuminated, but still he kept going.

More bumps, more field, and then a fence!

The fuel gauge was no longer working. The ABS light came on.

He kept going.

Next came the muffler, a shattered mess left in the middle of someone's yard.

But, Joe was almost at his destination. He could see the lights. His truck barreled on.

Focus on the mission.

Chapter 5

After they exited the alley, Williams and Bailey helped Marty behind a car across the street. Guthrie had his AR pointed downrange, but the shooter was nowhere to be seen. Marty wasn't as concerned about the shooter, however, as he was about his wounds.

He looked down and saw that blood was quickly beginning to pool beneath his lower left leg. Being a Marine and a police officer, Marty knew how to tell arterial blood from other types of blood. Arterial blood was highly oxygenated, making it bright red. The puddle beneath him was without a doubt a puddle of arterial blood, and he knew he didn't have much time.

He reached into his vest looking for his tourniquet, but he couldn't find it. Where was it? He was growing a bit frantic as he searched. Then he remembered: it was in his SWAT vest back at the station.

"Toss me a first aid kit!" he hollered at Bailey.

Bailey got into the police car and grabbed a kit for him. Marty searched through it.

No tourniquet.

The best he could find was an H-bandage. That would have to do.

He began to wrap it around his leg just below his knee, but it didn't take long for it to snap. He tossed it to the side and moved on to his last option: he would have to find the bullet hole and stick his finger in it.

His body was freezing in the summer heat. He was fading in and out, like in the early hours of the morning when you keep hitting the snooze button. Somewhat there, somewhat not.

He reached down to his calf and started searching for the bullet hole; he had to stop the bleeding now or he was a goner. He rubbed his hands all over his skin all the way down to his ankle. He couldn't find it. He finally used what little energy he had left to lift his head just a tiny bit more so he could see his feet, and that's when he saw it. Or, rather, that's when he saw next to nothing.

His left foot was over half gone; the force behind the bullet had blown it apart. There was no way to stop the bleeding without a tourniquet or functioning H-bandage. There was nothing to be done in that moment.

He needed an ambulance, and he needed it now.

His backup had called for one; Marty knew this. Help would be there soon.

Just as he thought on this, he saw the lights of an ambulance down the street. A rush of relief overwhelmed him as he and the other officers waved at the ambulance.

But it didn't budge.

The medics could see him; he knew they could see him! That's when Marty realized what was really going on: the medics wouldn't come for him. They most likely had orders from above them to not enter the hot zone. Though it was a logical policy, Marty struggled to understand it in that moment. He was *dying*. He was dying and the people that should be coming to his rescue were sitting in a fully-equipped ambulance down the street. He felt hopeless.

The cold began to spread all over his body; even his insides felt like they were frozen as he laid his head down on the concrete. He looked up to the stars again, his constant source of light in the constant darkness, the now growing darkness.

He looked to the left and made a note of the street sign: Water and East. This was where he was going to die. The corner of Water and East.

He then returned his attention to the stars. He was thankful that he would die on a clear, summer night. The stars seem so much more beautiful when you know that they're the last things you're going to see. They were magnificent witnesses to what would likely be his final thoughts.

Despite the fact that he had been in dangerous situations numerous times throughout his life, he had never planned what his last thoughts would be. When you have a career that places you in situations that threaten your life, you can't allow yourself to think about death. When you think on it, it has power over you. You must maintain power over death, or at least maintain the mindset that you do. It's the only way to remain sane.

We all watch television shows and movies wherein warriors, ancient and modern, die fighting honorably on the battlefield. Do you ever wonder though, reader, what their final thoughts were? Maybe you never have, or maybe you have once or twice. Or maybe you're a deep, emotional thinker who ponders mortality and the human condition, and maybe you've looked at these warriors lying on the grass and thought, "What are they thinking about?" Their blood pooling beneath them, the sounds of battle around them growing muffled, and their vision darkening more and more with each passing moment. What is going through their minds?

As Marty lay dying, there was only one thought going through his mind. It overpowered his pain, the cold, the darkness; this one thought was echoing off of the walls of his consciousness and aggressively demanding an answer.

"Did I kiss my kids and tell them how much I love them?"

Had he? Had he done these things before he left for work that night? He couldn't remember. He tried so desperately to remember, but he simply could not.

The puddle of blood was growing larger. His body grew colder. The stars were fading.

He didn't have much consciousness left. This time had to be used wisely.

And he did what most people would do in a situation such as this: he prayed. Though, he didn't pray for himself. He didn't pray for God to intervene. He didn't pray for angels to swoop down from Heaven and wrap a tourniquet around his leg. He didn't pray for comfort. He didn't think of himself at all.

He prayed only for his children.

His son Ryan was 18 years old, his daughter Hayley was 14 and soon to be a sophomore in high school. Things had never been quite the same since he and their mother were divorced, especially between he and Hayley. He had done and said things he regretted, but he didn't think on those things in that moment.

His only thought, his only prayer was: "God, please let my children know how much I love them."

He hadn't always been the best father; he knew that. But, he hoped that his children knew how much they meant to him. He needed them to know that in his final moments, he thought only of them. He prayed only for them.

And with that prayer, he accepted his fate. The cold was overwhelming now. His vision was growing darker, but he wasn't afraid of the dark in that moment. How could he be afraid of the dark when the stars were watching over him so lovingly, so diligently?

"Marty!" a voice called.

He looked up to see Sergeant Nick Durr walking toward him. Marty had no idea where he had come from or when he had gotten there, but he was glad he was there. Durr knelt down and looked at Marty's foot.

"We're gonna get you some help," he said. "Let's take a look at that."

Suddenly, they were all overwhelmed with a horrendous sound. Marty abandoned the stars for a moment as he tilted his chin up in an attempt to look behind him. That's when he saw the headlights. A giant, hunk of junk truck was heading straight toward him.

"You've gotta be kidding me," he thought. "This lunatic ditched the gun, got in his truck, and decided to run over me to finish the job!"

The headlights drew closer and closer, the sound grew louder and louder. There was nothing he could do. He closed his eyes and waited for the inevitable.

But nothing happened. The loud noise quieted, and Marty dared to open his eyes.

The truck had stopped about 30 feet away, and somebody was walking toward him. He looked to the left as the figure approached, expecting to see a gun pointed at his face, but he saw something entirely unexpected.

He saw ugly ass Jerusalem cruiser sandals, blue jean shorts that were way too big, and a tie-dyed t-shirt, and he thought, "This is the *ugliest* angel I have *ever* seen!"

Chapter 6

It was a miracle that Joe had pulled up right where his brother lay bleeding out. He stood over his brother and examined him; he didn't look good.

"Joe, I've been shot," Marty explained.

Joe placed his hands on his hips and nodded his head.

"Yeah, I know. That's why I'm here."

Marty will tell anyone the following: "I hate Joe. I'll punch him right in the face if I get the chance. But when things are going south, there's nobody else I want by my side." Although he was happy to see his brother, they weren't out of the woods yet.

"The medics aren't coming," Marty explained. "It's a hot zone. I don't have a tourniquet."

Joe quickly took his belt off and wrapped it around his brother's leg. Marty groaned in agony as Joe pulled the belt tighter and tighter. This hurt worse than being shot!

"Alright, that'll have to do," Joe said. "Durr! We gotta get him into my truck!"

"What can I do to help?"

Joe whipped around and saw a large man in jeans and a t-shirt staring at him and anxiously awaiting an answer to his question.

"Who the hell are you?" Joe shouted.

Larry looked surprised and a little hurt.

"Joe, I'm your trash man," he replied.

Joe shook his head and threw his arms in the air.

"What is my trash man doing in the middle of a gun fight in Pendleton?"

"He's my ride-along," Marty answered.

There was no time to ask more questions. Joe figured that at least now he had another pair of hands to help.

"Okay Durr, we're gonna lift him into the back of the truck," he ordered. "Then Larry, you're going to lay behind him. You pull that belt tight and do not let up on it for *any* reason. Keep his leg elevated, too."

Everyone carried out Joe's commands swiftly and accurately. In any other situation, Marty may have felt a little strange getting spooned by his trash man, but given the fact that he was fading in and out of consciousness, he didn't think much on it.

22

"Alright guys," Joe said before he got into the driver's seat, "I only know one way outta here, and it's gonna be a bumpy ride. Everyone hold on tight."

He started up the truck and headed back out the way he came. As he drove through the fences and the bird feeder, he decided that he would take a moment to pray. God had been with him that night; that was plain. As he pulled out onto MLKJ Blvd, he began to say a prayer.

"God, please let me get him to the hospital in time. I know I'm not always the best person, but I'll do anything God, anything, if you just please save my brother."

"I'm sorry, Joe," a voice said.

Joe was surprised and, truthfully, a bit disappointed.

'Um, let's not be too quick to judge, God," he thought.

Just as he was wondering how in the world he had warranted an actual audible response from the Creator of the universe, Williams popped his head up from the back seat.

"Joe," he continued. "I think I've been shot!"

Joe didn't even have a moment to wonder how in the *world* Williams had ended up in the back seat of his truck; all he was focused on now was getting to the hospital.

"Well now's a hell of a time to tell me, Williams!" he shouted. "Put your finger in the hole and we'll be at the hospital soon!"

They were outside of Pendleton now, but they still had about six miles to go before they reached the hospital. As he zoomed down the road, Joe saw flashing lights in the distance. Not police lights, though, ambulance lights. There was an ambulance waiting for them along the side of the road.

Joe pulled over and looked up to the sky.

"Thank you," he whispered to God.

He got out of the car and was quickly greeted by three Anderson firefighters, James Harless, Robin Branch, and Eric Hutchison, and a rookie EMT he didn't know at the time, but who he would come to learn was named Ming Ling.

"He's been shot in the foot and he's losing blood fast," Joe hurriedly explained as he rushed with them to the back of the truck.

"We'll take it from here, Joe," Robin said. "It's gonna be okay. We've got him."

He didn't understand how they knew to meet him there, but he was grateful to see them. He would later come to learn that these men had heard about Marty's situation on the scanner while they were down at the station. They didn't see how it was right to just leave a fallen officer to die, so they decided to "commandeer" an ambulance.

Robin and Joe got Marty onto the gurney and wheeled him over to the ambulance. Joe looked at his little brother, growing paler, covered in blood, barely able to keep his eyes open. Marty was grown, yes, but all Joe saw was his baby brother. Just before they lifted him onto the ambulance, Marty's eyes began to close.

Joe slapped the shit out of him, and Marty's eyes flew open. His older brother pointed his finger right in his face and sent him off with a stern command.

"Not today!"

Chapter 7

As Marty was riding in the ambulance, all he could think was, "It's a complete LIE that adrenaline makes a gunshot not hurt! I feel like my lower half is in a bonfire!" He was in agony as one of the medics worked on getting an IV in his arm, but as soon as he got one and hit him with that first dose of morphine, he thought, "Hey, I can enjoy this ride!"

As they zoomed through downtown Anderson, the rookie EMT struggled to take Marty's left boot off. He tugged and tugged but to no avail, and though the morphine certainly helped, it wasn't strong enough to fight off the pain that the EMT was accidentally inflicting.

"Hey, kid, you're gonna rip my foot off!" Marty shouted.

The young man looked at him in shock as he gently laid Marty's foot back on the gurney. Before long, the ambulance slowed down, and the doors flung open to reveal an ambulance bay. Marty lay as still as stone as they lowered him out of the ambulance and into the bright lights of St. Vincent Anderson Regional Hospital Emergency Department.

This wasn't how he was used to entering the ED. He always used the ambulance bay, yes, but he was usually walking in with a person in handcuffs. Obtaining jail clearance was a necessity when arresting someone for a DUI or when a takedown got a little rough. It usually didn't take long, and he always enjoyed the chance to chat with the staff. The best nights, though, were when he showed up to obtain jail clearance and his brother was the officer monitoring the psych rooms. There was nothing better than a chance to annoy his brother while he was working.

This trip to the ED was clearly much different. Marty was surrounded by people from the moment they wheeled him into the trauma hallway. Nurses, techs, radiology techs, respiratory therapists, registration staff, a phlebotomist, a pharmacist; he was the most popular guy in the hospital! He recognized most of the faces. These were his acquaintances, his friends. He took comfort in knowing that he was in the best of hands.

When they wheeled him into the trauma room, he knew he was probably going to have to feel a little more pain.

"Alright sir," the EMT said, "We have to move you onto the bed."

Marty held his breath as a team of people slid him from the gurney onto the bed; it didn't hurt as bad as he thought it would. That morphine was good stuff.

A nurse explained to him that the next thing they had to do was to cut all his clothes off. And yes, that included his underwear, to his distress and dismay. As he felt the legs off his pants fall away, a nurse began to wipe the blood off of his face with a wet washcloth. This was his only chance, and he was determined to take it.

"Hey," he began. "Listen, I know pretty much all of you, and I gotta come back in here eventually and face all of you. Now, those ladies down there are about to cut off my underwear, and they're all gonna see what I'm working with, and they're gonna know I'm a liar."

The nurse couldn't help but chuckle as she finished wiping the blood from his cheek. She grabbed another washcloth from the counter, folded it in half twice, and gently placed it over "what he was working with". He let out a sigh of relief.

"Thank you," he said with a slight grin.

He was so distracted by this mission that he hadn't realized one of the nurses was busy trying to get his left boot off. He only realized it when she successfully removed it and asked, "Um, is that a bullet?"

The bullet that had been trapped in his boot had fallen to the blood-splattered floor.

"Save that for evidence," another nurse ordered.

Marty was completely naked now as the doctor was busy examining every inch of his body. They checked his pupils, his airways, and several other things as he stared at the ceiling thinking of nothing at all in this fog of morphine. Everyone in the room was busy doing something, and it seemed like chaos to him, but everything was done in perfect order. Every person knew their task.

"Is that another bullet hole?" the doctor asked.

He shouldn't have done it; he knew he shouldn't have done it. Why he did it, who knows? But Marty had to see for himself. He used all his strength to lift his head and look down at his legs, and that's when he realized how bad things were.

His left foot looked even worse in this bright lighting. Aside from his toes, a couple ligaments, and a part of his heel, it had all been blown away by the sheer force of the bullet. He also remembered then that he had been shot in the right leg, as well. He laid his head back down as the severity of his situation truly set in.

"Let's get him ready for StatFlight," the doctor ordered.

This was good and bad. It was good because it meant that he was going to survive, but it was bad because it meant that things were really, really serious. Nobody gets flown to Indianapolis unless he's in bad shape. But, at least he had a good chance of following Joe's orders.

Not today!

He wasn't going to die today.

He didn't stay at the hospital long enough for anyone to really visit. The StatFlight team was ready to go in less than half an hour; he needed to be in Indy as soon as was humanly possible. He vaguely remembered speaking with his niece, Cara, as they wheeled him to the elevator to the helipad, but even that seemed more like a dream than reality because of the morphine. However, the loss of the memories was a small price to pay for relief from the extreme pain.

The helicopter ride seemed like a dream to him, as well. As the helicopter banked to the left, he was able to gaze out the window and see a spectacle of blue and red flashing lights in Pendleton. He knew Joe was down there somewhere seeking justice for his little brother, mercilessly hunting down this criminal. The view lasted only for a moment though, and soon they were headed straight for St. Vincent Indianapolis.

When the helicopter landed in Indy, the StatFlight crew wheeled him down a hallway toward the trauma center. The hallway was lined with Indianapolis police officers, and each one offered a show of support. Some touched his hand while others used words to encourage and strengthen him.

"How did they find out?" he wondered.

Word of a fallen officer spread fast; he knew this. He just didn't realize *how* fast until that night.

He would later reflect on how beautiful it was to see so many of his law enforcement brothers and sisters supporting him. He was in a scary place, and he was about to go under the knife, and who knew what the outcome would be? Nobody but God knew for certain. And one of the last things he saw before he went back to get prepped for surgery was an incredible outpouring of love and support.

They hastily wheeled him down the hall. He had been given more morphine at some point, though he couldn't remember when. He could tell, though, because he felt amazing, and because he couldn't focus. Things were happening so fast that he couldn't keep up. He was confused, voices speaking to him and making no sense.

He was wheeled into a room where nurses began preparing him for surgery. It would be a little while before they could get him back, an hour or so. If his family got there in time, he could see them for a moment.

He breathed a sigh of relief. Not only would he live to see his family again, he might get to see them before he goes under the knife. He stared at the ceiling and thanked the Lord above.

Things were going to be okay.

Chapter 8

Fallujah, Iraq between 2003 and 2006 was not an enjoyable place to be. This is putting it mildly, of course. A better way to explain it would be hell on Earth, a place where explosions and gunfire rang through the desert air day in and day out. The Second Battle of Fallujah, or Operation Phantom Fury, as it was code-named, was a joint U.S., British, and Iraqi offensive to take control of the city which was at the time occupied by insurgents.

Joe Garrett was 46 years old when he was stationed in Fallujah. He was part of Operation Iraqi Freedom 1, 2, and 3, an operation that relieved the men and women in Operation Phantom Fury and focused on keeping Fallujah out of the hands of insurgents. Joe had been deployed more times since he was in the Reserves than he ever had when he was on active duty. That was just sometimes the way of things, though, and Joe did what he could to make the best of it. It wasn't a fun place to be, but he was a Marine, a warrior. He would do whatever it took to complete the mission.

The thing about being stationed in a place as volatile as Fallujah was that you could be talking to a guy one minute, and he would be gone the next. There were reminders of this often, but one day brought an incredibly deep, hurtful reminder to Joe.

Joe received care packages often; most of the Marines did. Joe being Joe, however, he didn't care much for the comforts of home when he was trying to focus on the mission, on being a warrior. So, he would always ask for something that he knew he didn't want, but that the Iraqi children would want: Dum-Dums. These little suckers held up well in the desert heat, and Joe enjoyed the smiles that emerged on the children's faces as he passed the candies out to them downtown. It was a small ray of hope in an otherwise dismal place.

One day in November, Joe received a care package that had, as he had requested, a package of Dum-Dums. He was speaking with an Iraqi First Sergeant as he opened it. The man spoke of his kids at home, and how good they were when he was away. Joe handed him the bag of suckers with instructions to give them to his kids back home. The man smiled and thanked him for his kindness as he shoved the bag into the pocket on the leg of his pants before heading on his way.

As was usual in Fallujah, the peace did not last for long. Five minutes after this conversation, there was an explosion down the street. Joe and others in his unit quickly responded to try to save any that could be saved. When they reached the wreckage, Joe grabbed onto a leg that was sticking out of the rubble. He pulled and pulled until, suddenly, the pant leg ripped, and at Joe's feet were dozens of Dum-Dums.

At Camp Fallujah in December of 2005, Joe and other members of the US and Iraqi forces took a small break from the chaos to attend a memorial service for the US and Iraqi lives lost in all of the battles in Fallujah. It was an emotional experience for all involved, but the day would prove to be life-changing for him.

At the conclusion of the memorial service, Joe made his way to one of the blue porta potties to gather his thoughts. If you've never seen the inside of a porta potty on a military base, you should know that it is covered in more writing than any middle school bathroom in America. As Joe was trying to pull himself together, he decided to read some of the wisdom from these great philosophers that graced the walls with their musings. Most of these musings involved someone or another liking "the D", but Joe was taken back by one in particular. One short musing that would change his entire outlook on life.

Born to die… just not today

Admittedly, Joe had been struggling for a while with the battle and the war in general. Joe was a few years shy of fifty, and he was still alive. It was young people who weren't getting to go home. He asked himself every single day, "Why are these kids dying?"

He had known two of the young men who were being memorialized that day. They were kids to him, kids whose lives had barely begun. And he struggled with that. But as he stared at those words on the porta potty wall, he began to understand.

We are all going to die; that is a fact. No person on Earth can escape this fate. But, we have the choice to fight. We have the choice to look death in the face and say, "Not today. You're not taking me without a fight."

That was what Joe realized that day. Those words were the seed that would eventually grow into the Warrior Mindset. You focus on the mission, you utilize common sense, you refuse to die without a fight, (and) you remember that God is in control. There is no place for fear.

After that day, that revelation, Joe began to enjoy his time in Iraq. He saw it as a paid vacation, with the exception of the times that he was getting shot at. He swam in the Euphrates River. He went fishing. He laid out under the stars; every night was a clear night because the intense heat didn't allow for any cloud cover.

And in everything he did, in everything he does, those words ring through his head in a peaceful, reassuring tune.

Born to die… just not today

These words rang through his head as he watched the ambulance that was carrying his brother speed down the road. He had probably slapped Marty a little too hard, but he was just so afraid that he wasn't going to open his eyes again, and that wasn't how he wanted to remember his baby brother.

"So, what are we going to do now?" Larry asked, breaking the silence.

Joe looked at him and answered without hesitation.

"We're going back to Pendleton so I can find this guy!"

A look of passionate anger emerged on Larry's face, and he nodded his head in agreement.

"Yes!" he shouted. "Let's go!"

He turned around and ran toward the truck. He was in the passenger seat with his seatbelt fastened before Joe reached the door. Though Joe was still completely focused on the mission, he couldn't help but allow a stray thought to pop into his head:

"Wow, our trashman is kind of a badass."

Larry had already shown incredible bravery. He didn't have to go out into the hot zone earlier. He didn't have to hold Marty's tourniquet and get tossed around in the back of a truck speeding over bumpy ground and broken fences. And he didn't have to hop into the passenger seat and head back to Pendleton with Joe. He didn't have to do any of it, but he did. He put himself in harm's way to help a fallen officer, to help a friend. And if you don't think that's badass, then you probably have an uncool trashman and you're just jealous.

As he drove back to Pendleton, Joe knew that he needed to let somebody know about Marty. He called the one person he knew would still be up: his 20-year-old daughter, Cara. Thankfully, she answered the phone.

"Cara, wake up your mom. Tell her to go get your grandparents and head to the hospital."

"Wait, what?" she asked.

"Marty's been shot, but I just talked to him. The dog's dead. I'm gonna kill this son of a bitch. That's all I can tell you. I've gotta go."

Chapter 9

Joe's wife, Mendy, was slightly concerned when she heard her phone ringing late on the night of July 26th, 2012. She saw that her daughter Cara was trying to call her, and she knew it couldn't be for a good reason. She thought that perhaps she had a flat tire or was locked out of her car. She was only 20, after all, and at that age, don't we all still rely on our parents for some things? When she answered the phone, however, she knew that this was something far worse.

"Mom," Cara said through tears. "Uncle Marty's been shot. Dad's trying to get ahold of you."

She wasn't able to respond for a few moments. Had she really just heard what she thought she heard? Was she dreaming? Surely she must have been dreaming. But as she heard her daughter sobbing, she realized that no, this was real. This was happening.

"Where are you?" she asked.

"On my way home from work."

"Go straight to the hospital," she said. "I'm going to call your dad."

She tried to call her husband as quickly as possible, but her hands were shaking. When she finally managed it, Joe picked up right away and told her that Marty had been shot in the foot and that Kilo was dead.

"I need you to go pick up mom and dad and head to St. Vincent."

Mendy had so many questions. How serious was the injury? Was Marty going to be okay? Are *you* okay? But she knew that now wasn't the time. She had been married to Joe for 15 years, and she could tell when he was on a mission, when he was fully engaged in the Warrior Mindset. She simply said that she would do what he asked, and got off the phone.

She told their 18-year-old son Kegan to stay at home with their two youngest daughters, 8-year-old Sophie and 6-year-old Ava, before throwing on some clothes and running to the car. Thankfully, they only lived down the road from Joe's parents. As she drove, she thought about how she would tell them. There was no easy way to say these things; she knew his mother would panic. She decided that she would stop by Joe's other brother Mark's house and have him go with her. He could help her keep his parents calm. She needed help desperately.

He didn't live far out of the way at all either, and she whipped into the driveway and ran to the front door. Mark's wife, Janeen, answered the door and stared at her in shock.

"Mendy," she said, "what's wrong?"

"Marty's been shot in the foot," Mendy explained. "Is Mark here? I need him to go with me to get Irene and JB."

Janeen immediately began to panic, as well.

"Mark's not home," she answered.

Mark was a hard worker, just like his brothers. It wasn't unusual for him to work late, but Mendy grew even more dismayed.

"Alright," Mendy replied. "Well, you're coming with me!"

Her sister-in-law was hesitant, but Mendy's tone told her that it wasn't optional. The two women got into the car and zoomed down the road to Joe's parents' house. When they arrived, Mendy opened the car door, but Janeen stayed where she was.

"I can't go in!" she sobbed. "I'm going to get sick!"

Though Mendy was usually a sympathetic person, her stores of sympathy were running short that night. She, like her husband, was on a mission.

"Oh yes you *are* going in with me," she argued, "because I can't hold both of them up by myself."

Janeen acquiesced and got out of the car, but she didn't make it to the front porch before beginning to puke in the yard. Mendy left her there and started pounding on the door. She did this for a couple of minutes before giving up and getting back into the car. The two women decided that all they could do was just head to the hospital.

As they got further down the road, however, they saw Irene, Joe's mother, at the same stop sign as them heading home from work. Mendy quickly stopped the car and hopped out to flag her down. She was successful in this endeavor.

"Irene!" she practically shouted as she jogged up the window. "Irene, you need to come with me. Marty's been shot in the foot."

She tried really hard to emphasize the word "foot" in an attempt to stop Irene from panicking, but it was a failed attempt. Irene began screaming and crying, and no matter how many times Mendy told her that he was shot in the foot and that it probably wasn't that bad, she couldn't stop crying.

"Irene, you need to follow me back to your house so we can get JB," she ordered. "We have to go."

Irene did as she was told, but she was in hysterics the whole time. When they arrived at the house and woke JB, Irene's husband and Joe, Marty, and Mark's dad, he was surprised, but able to maintain his composure. When everybody was in the car, Janeen began to cry once again.

"Take me home, Mendy," she cried. "Please. I need Mark to go instead of me. I can't do this."

Mendy did her best to comfort Janeen as they drove back to her house. By Divine intervention, it worked out perfectly that this had happened. When Mendy pulled into Janeen's driveway, Mark parked along the side of the road. He had just returned home from work, and the shock was evident on his face.

"Mendy, what's going on?" he asked as he met her outside her car.

She explained what had happened and what she knew, which admittedly wasn't a whole lot.

"We'll take my car, but you're driving," she ordered as she headed toward the vehicle.

She turned back around to see him still standing there staring at her.

"Let's go!" she shouted.

This seemed to jolt Mark into action, and he quickly followed his sister-in-law's orders.

As they headed toward Anderson, nobody said a word. They were all confused and scared. Though they understood why Joe couldn't give them all anymore details, it was frustrating to be left in the dark. There were so many questions and absolutely no answers.

The drive seemed to all to last for an eternity, but when they finally reached Anderson, Mendy's phone began to ring. It was Cara.

"Mom, they're flying Marty to St. Vincent in Indy," she said. "I got to talk to him for a second, but they had to go."

"We'll meet you there," she replied. "It's going to be okay."

She hung up and told everyone what was happening. Irene burst into tears once again, and Mendy decided that there was probably no way to console her at this point, but she tried anyway. She told her that Marty was going to the best hospital around, that he would be in great hands. But, in the back of her mind, all she could think was, "This is bad. This is really bad."

She called the one person she always turned to when she needed help: her sister, Yvonne Burt.

"Hello?"

Mendy breathed a sigh of relief at the sound of her sister's voice. She told her everything that had happened, and Yvonne immediately knew just how to comfort her.

"I'm heading there now, Mendy," she said. "I'll see how I can help out." Yvonne was an RN at St Vincent Indianapolis, and she was actually scheduled to work the next morning, but she didn't care about that. Her little sister was more important than sleep.

"Thank you," Mendy sighed. "I'll see you soon."

She felt a sense of calm rush over her as she hung up. Things were chaotic, yes, but she would have her sister with her. She took a deep breath and gathered her strength. She wasn't going to fall apart.

Not today.

Chapter 10

Back in Middletown, Marty's fiancée, Jess, was busy doing laundry. It was one of many things on her list of tasks to accomplish before their wedding in two weeks. She wanted the house to be spotless; one less thing to stress her out before the big day.

She thought that she would probably head to bed after her next load, but she hated to go to bed without talking to Marty. They usually talked on the phone a few times a night when he was on shift. He would call her after roll call, she would call him before bed, she would call him if she woke up in the middle of the night; it was their usual schedule. Though there were of course times when he couldn't answer, he would always call her back. She never cared if it woke her up. She just wanted to hear his voice. She just wanted to know that he was safe.

She had tried to call him over an hour ago, though not for a cutesy, romantic reason. She had just opened their phone bill and saw that he had overage charges for his text messages; one more stress to deal with before the wedding.

As she finished folding her load of laundry, she decided that she would try to call him again. Usually if he was busy, it would ring for a minute or so before going to voicemail. This time, however, it went straight to voicemail.

"Huh, that's weird," she mumbled to herself.

She convinced herself that it was probably just a glitch. Marty never turned his phone off, and he would never let it die while he was on duty. No chance.

She called again, and it did the same thing. A wave of worry began to rush over her as she stared at her phone.

"Jess?"

She turned around to see Marty's son, Ryan, standing in the hallway. He was on the verge of tears, a look of panic plastered on his face.

"Jess, what just happened?" he asked.

"What are you talking about?" she replied.

"Somebody just texted me and said that they saw on Facebook that dad and Kilo had been hurt. What's going on?"

Her worry turned to panic as she frantically called Marty again.

Voicemail.

She did the only thing she could think to do: she called dispatch.

A woman answered the phone and Jess quickly explained who she was.

"I've heard Marty and Kilo have been hurt!" Jess practically yelled.

"Oh, yes," the woman replied. "They've both been shot."

Jess felt like she could vomit. Her heart began to race.

"Are they alive? What happened?"

"I heard Marty on the radio," the woman answered. "That's all I know."

Jess was somewhere between frantic and pissed off. That's all the lady knew? She so nonchalantly told her that the love of her life had been shot and she couldn't even say if he was alive or not?

"Well, I need to get to the hospital," she snapped.

"Ma'm, you probably shouldn't be driving in this state."

Jess felt her blood begin to boil.

"Then send someone to come get me!" she shouted.

"There is nobody," the woman replied. "I'm sorry. They're all responding to the shooting."

Jess was in tears now. She hung up the phone and looked at Ryan who was staring at her with a blank look on his face.

"Can you drive us?" she asked through sobs.

He nodded his head and quickly grabbed the car keys.

"Let's go," he said.

As they hopped in the car, Jess' phone began to ring. She reached into her purse to grab it, praying to God that it was Marty. But, it wasn't. It was Marty's fourteen-year-old daughter, Hayley.

"Hayley," she said.

"Jess!" she responded. "I just saw on Facebook that dad and Kilo have been shot! Is it true?"

"Yes, Ryan and I are on our way to get you."

Hayley was at her mother's house, which thankfully wasn't out of the way. When they picked her up, they all headed down the main road of town straight for Anderson. However, before they got out of Middletown, they saw Middletown K9 Officer, Mike Vaccaro, parked alongside the road.

"Pull over!" Jess ordered Ryan.

He did as she was told, and Jess hopped out of the car and walked up to Mike's vehicle. He rolled down the window once he recognized who it was.

"Jess," he said.

"Marty's been shot," she sobbed.

She really didn't understand why she had told Ryan to stop or what she expected Mike to do.

"I heard," he replied. "I'm waiting for clearance to go to Pendleton and assist."

Jess stood there and continued to sob, and he rubbed his neck and sighed.

"You know what? Forget it. I'm going, and I'm gonna get someone to escort you to the hospital."

It didn't take more than a couple minutes for a Middletown Reserve car to show up with sirens blaring. Ryan followed behind him all the way to St. Vincent Anderson. When they pulled into the parking lot, they saw the helicopter taking off. Jess ran through the ER doors and saw Cara standing in the waiting room.

"Cara!" she shouted.

She threw herself into her soon-to-be niece's arms and continued to cry.

"I just talked to him," Cara whispered in her ear, trying to comfort her. "I just talked to him. He was shot in the foot and the leg. He's going to Indy so they can do surgery. It's going to be okay. I talked to him."

Jess allowed herself to feel a bit of relief at Cara's words, but she still wanted to see him. She wanted to hold his hand and kiss him and tell him how much she loved him.

She loved him so much.

"Kilo didn't make it, though," Cara continued. "I'm sorry."

Her heart sank at this news. Kilo was a good dog, a loyal dog. He was more than just Marty's partner, he was their family's protector, their best friend.

Hayley and Ryan walked in the doors next and saw their cousin holding Jess.

"I just talked to him, guys," Cara said to them.

"We have to get to Indy," Jess said. "We have to go."

"One of the APD officers is going to drive you guys himself," Cara informed her. "I'll meet you there."

Jess nodded her head and wiped the tears from her face. It was going to be okay; she had to believe that.

She couldn't lose him, not now. They were two weeks away from their happily ever after. Two weeks away from starting the rest of their lives.

No, she wasn't going to lose him. He wasn't allowed to die.

Not today.

Chapter 11

Joe was almost to Pendleton by the time he got off the phone with his wife. He had complete confidence that she would take care of things back home. Now he could focus on the mission.

As he got closer to the scene, two county police officers started waving at him from the side of the road. Joe slowed down to see what they wanted.

"Yeah!" one of them shouted. "Go get that son of a bitch!"

Joe couldn't help but roll his eyes.

"Hey, you guys are missing one hell of a gunfight down here!" he shouted back.

Joe picked up speed and continued on his way. When they got back to the scene, he put the truck in park and looked at Larry.

Larry knew he wasn't going to be handed a gun to go in looking for the guy, of course, but he hoped that he would be able to help in some way. However, Joe instructed him to remain in the truck until he came back for him. Joe admired Larry's bravery, but he wouldn't be able to forgive himself if harm came to him. And besides, it's not smart to take civilians on a search and destroy mission.

That's what this was, after all. Joe suspected that the shooter wouldn't allow himself to be taken alive, not after he had shot a police officer. The guy had to understand the severity of the punishment that would be inflicted upon him in a court of law for his heinous act.

After Joe made sure Larry was out of harm's way, he started to walk up to parked police cars and turn off their sirens. The lights were enough; they didn't need the loud, unnecessary noises adding to the pandemonium. As he reached into one of the cars, a man popped his head out of the rolled down window.

"Get me out of here!" the man yelled.

"Shit!" Joe shouted.

Joe stared at the man in complete shock. When he finally realized that it was just a civilian ride-along trapped in the hot zone and *not* somebody trying to kill him, he let out an exasperated sigh.

"Okay, listen, my truck is parked down the street. My trashman is in there. Go tell him who you are and tell him I told you guys to wait there for me. Do NOT get out of the vehicle until I come back for you!"

The man frantically nodded his head as he exited the car and took off down the road.

Now that that random issue had been resolved, Joe joined a group of officers at the perimeter. Their Sergeant had pulled Guthrie out of the search in order to debrief the officers who were just arriving, since he was most familiar with the situation. Truthfully, though, nobody knew a whole lot. Nobody knew who the shooter was or why he was doing this. Not that he needed a reason, though; some people just shoot people to shoot people.

All they knew was that the Pendleton officer who had been shot had managed to get to safety; they wouldn't have to search for him, at least. And he wasn't injured too badly; he had only been grazed on the top of the leg. They did, however, have to consider the possibility of other undiscovered victims and/or potential hostages.

When Guthrie noticed that Joe had joined the group, he paused. Everyone at APD knew how strong the bond was between Marty and Joe. They knew that although they gave each other hell, they were inseparable. And they all knew that Joe would destroy anyone who dared to harm his baby brother. Joe was allowed to tell Marty that their parents were dead, he was allowed to jump out from dark places and scare him, he was allowed to give him wedgies and torment him, but nobody else was allowed to hurt his brother. Nobody.

Guthrie knew this, and that's why no words needed to be exchanged. He removed his AR from around his body and handed it to Joe with a simple nod of the head. Joe took it from him slowly and looked to the other officers. Their faces all said the same thing: go get him.

Joe marched inside the perimeter and began his mission. He didn't have a specific plan. This wasn't like Fallujah where everything was thought out and calculated. All he knew was that he needed to find this guy for two reasons: 1. To get justice for his brother and 2. To make sure he didn't hurt anybody else.

But Joe had no intel to go on. If he had known who the shooter was or what sort of mission he was on, perhaps he could have gone in with a better plan. But he knew nothing. He knew the guy had tried to kill a police officer, and had killed a police canine. That was all.

As Joe marched deeper into the perimeter, he felt the Warrior Mindset's grasp grow tighter and tighter. That mindset was his saving grace, and the greatest gift his Creator could have ever given him. He was grateful for

Fallujah, grateful for his struggle and his suffering. It had led him to this night, prepared him for this night.

He was ready to do what was necessary. He felt no fear. He was not going to die.

Not today.

Chapter 12

As soon as the police car pulled up to the hospital, Jess quickly thanked the officer and rushed through the doors. The woman at the front desk immediately took her back to the surgery waiting room with a promise that one of the surgery staff would be with her shortly. They didn't have to wait long before someone showed up, but it wasn't one of the surgery staff. It was a police officer.

He handed Jess Marty's badge, dirty and covered in his blood. She wanted to burst into tears at the sight of it, but she was interrupted by a voice.

"You're Officer Dulworth's family?"

A woman in scrubs was standing behind the police officer.

"Yes," Jess frantically replied. "Yes!"

"He's about to go back to surgery and he's on a lot of pain medicine, so he probably won't make much sense, but you can see him."

She felt a couple tears of joy escape as she nodded her head. She handed the badge to Ryan, and he and Hayley took a seat in the waiting room. She followed the nurse down the hallway and into the room where Marty lay waiting to go back to the operating room.

He was gray, a shell of the man that she was used to looking at. But the moment he looked at his fiance's face, his eyes lit up.

"Hey, babe," he hoarsely whispered.

She knelt down and grabbed his hand. She laid her head next to his on the pillow and continued to cry.

"Hey, hey, hey," he said. "I'm okay. Look! I'm here. It's okay, babe. It's all gonna be okay."

She squeezed his hand tighter and lifted her head. As she stared into his eyes, she saw how calm he appeared and she tried to appear the same, but she couldn't. She was so shaken by how close she had come to losing the love of her life, her best friend, her partner. Tears continued to slide down her cheeks, but he just grinned.

"I love you so much," he said.

"I love you, too," she replied.

She kissed him softly, and stared into his eyes for a few moments longer.

"Ryan and Hayley are here," she said. "I'll send them in."

He grasped her hand tighter. He didn't want her to leave, but he also wanted to see his children. He so badly wanted to see his children. He nodded his head, and she gave him one more kiss before going to grab them.

Ryan, Hayley, and Irene and JB got to talk to Marty before he went to surgery, though not for very long. The surgeon had to get the artery repaired and pack the wound before infection began to set in. After the surgical staff wheeled him away, the family gathered in the waiting room. And although most of them had gotten to speak with Marty, they were still on edge.

"We should all sit down and try to relax," Mendy said. "We need to catch our breath."

There were plenty of people taking care of things for them. Yvonne was staying on top of all things medical, asking questions nobody would have thought to ask and explaining the medical terminology to everyone. The Chaplain was in the waiting room with them, available for prayer should the desire arise in any of the family members. And several police officers were there, as well, saying little but standing in solidarity with this law enforcement family. The family was receiving an incredible amount love and support, though their worry still overpowered them.

After a few minutes passed by, Cara's anxious curiosity drove her to turn on the news. There was some coverage on the situation, but nobody really knew what was going on. The coverage was vague and unhelpful, but they kept it on just in case something new was said.

As they waited for news of Marty, every person was lost in their own thoughts, or their own regrets.

Jess thought of how mad she had been about that phone bill. What if she had called him before the shooting? She was thankful that he didn't have to hear her be so angry right before going through such a terrifying and painful experience.

She thought about how he had wanted to take the night off. God, why didn't she just let him take the night off? He could have been sleeping in bed next to her right now, not lying underneath a knife. She began to cry again.

Hayley was busy thinking about the last conversation she had had with her father before he left for work that night. They had been fighting; they fought a lot those days. It seemed they could never see eye to eye on anything. The last phone conversation they had was earlier that day, and she had hung up on him. He had made her so angry that she hung up on him, and she cursed herself for doing it. What if he had died in that alley? Did he think about that while he lay there bleeding out? She tried to banish the thoughts from her head, but she couldn't.

Irene thought of her baby boy. Being the mother of police officers is not an easy task, and though one might think that it grows easier with time, it doesn't. She always worried, but she always tried to remind herself that plenty of police officers never get shot. They always return home. That was how she coped with it. She prayed, and she told herself these things.

Well, she now realized then that these things can happen to anyone. Her family wasn't immune. Her baby boy wasn't immune. She figured that all she really had left was prayer, but that was enough for her. It would always be enough.

She also thought about Joe. He had always been Marty's protector, even if he did torment his little brother every now and then. Joe had a soldier's mentality, and that terrified her. She looked at the clock on the wall, and she felt her panic creep back in.

"Why isn't Joe here yet?" she asked as the tears welled up again. "He needs to be here with his family."

Cara started to open her mouth to say that there was no way Joe would come back until that guy was dead or arrested, to share what her father had told her on the phone, but she decided not to. It was something that everybody already knew, anyway.

"I'll call dispatch," Mendy said. "They've already sent guys out to get him, though, Irene. He won't listen."

"Well, get me the Chief's number then," she said. "We'll make him come back!"

Hayley and Ryan looked at their cousin, and she shrugged her shoulders. That might get her father to leave the scene, and it might not. Her father was a warrior that sometimes could not be talked down.

Mendy set about getting in contact with the Chief. It was decided that she would do the talking, as Irene was still too distraught. Mendy told him that Joe's mother was very upset and worried, and that she couldn't survive it if she lost two of her three sons in one night. She told him that his mother wanted him here with his family.

The Chief assured her that he would do all he could to get Joe to leave the scene. She thanked him, but she didn't have full confidence that he would succeed. However, she hoped he would. Because like her mother-in-law, she wanted Joe there, too. She wanted her husband to be safe.

She said a prayer for Joe, and she said a prayer for the Chief.

Chapter 13

Joe had been searching for over an hour before the first Anderson police officers were sent out to retrieve him.

"You need to come back, Joe," they had told him. "You should be with your family."

Joe ever so kindly told them that he wasn't leaving the scene until he knew that the son of a bitch was captured or dead, and that they could go tell that to anybody who wanted him to leave. He didn't have time to sympathize with his family; he couldn't. He was in the Warrior Mindset. He was going to make this guy pay for what he had done no matter how long he had to be out there.

The night sky reminded him of Fallujah. He remembered how hopeless he felt watching his brothers die on the battlefield, how confused and disillusioned he was. And though he remembered those feelings very well, he couldn't feel them anymore. He wouldn't allow himself to feel them anymore. Because his brother wasn't going to die, and he wasn't going to fail. Justice would be served. This guy wasn't going to win. Not today.

He searched through a large portion of the perimeter. He searched in yards and behind trees and under cars. For another two hours he searched, all the while people begging him to come back to the perimeter.

Joe wouldn't hear of that. He wouldn't hear of giving up. It wasn't in his nature.

He left the perimeter once to try to get some updates; his radio was dead by this point. There was no news, so he got right back to it.

In the third hour, he began to think that he would never find the guy. Had he escaped the perimeter? How could he have? No, no he couldn't have. There was no way. That perimeter was set up quickly and locked down tight. He called out to the shooter over and over again trying to get him to come out. Had he killed himself? That would be a suitable outcome.

Was he holed up somewhere with a hostage? That was Joe's biggest fear; that was everyone's biggest fear. Though Joe wanted justice to be served, what he wanted most was to stop the unnecessary violence and loss of life. That was what he was trained to do: protect people. And that was what fueled everything he did.

Eventually, Sergeant Durr found him and tried to break him out of the Warrior Mindset.

"Joe," he said, "your wife called the Chief. She said your mom really wants you at the hospital with the rest of the family. She's a mess."

Joe groaned. He couldn't believe that they were playing the "mom card" on him! However, it was then that he allowed himself to think of his family. He thought about how scared they must be. He had hardly told them anything, he had given them no words of comfort because of his rush to get justice. They had spent the past few hours in a state of confusion and uncertainty and fear while he put himself in harm's way.

He thought about his mom and how upset she must be that one son had been shot and another was marching around a hot zone with an AR. She must have been hysterical at the thought of losing two of her three sons in one night.

He thought of Cara and how terrified she sounded on the phone. There's no task more sacred in this world than protecting one's own children, and that also includes comforting them when they need you.

And he thought of his wife. She was a strong woman, and he knew that she was holding everything together. Her strength was one of the reasons he loved her so much. But he knew that she wanted him there, too. Nobody had to tell him that part.

He looked up at the stars once again. The Iraqi man to whom he had given the Dum-Dums that day in 2005, he didn't get to go home to his family that day. He died as a warrior, and it was an honorable death. Joe knew that he wasn't going to die that day; he had already decided that. But as he thought about his family, the people he loved most in this world, he knew that they didn't have that same surety. They were worried, and he felt guilty.

He sighed and nodded his head

"Okay," he told Durr. "Let's go."

As they walked to the edge of the perimeter, Joe handed the AR off to an officer that only had a 9mm. When he reached the area where he had parked his truck, he was greeted by his APD brothers. He was frustrated that he hadn't found the shooter, but he knew that APD would find the man and serve justice. As he walked back to his truck, he noticed that the windows were all fogged up. He had completely forgotten that he had put Larry and the other man in there over three hours ago!

He knocked on the window, and Larry slowly cracked it.

"Who is it?" he asked.

"It's Joe! Roll down the damn window!"

Larry did as he was told, and he stared at Joe with a look of extreme pain.

"Joe! Thank goodness!" he yelled. "Is it okay if we pee real quick?"

"Yeah, yeah, go ahead," Joe replied with a wave of his hand.

The two men practically jumped out of the car and ran to the open field. Joe could've sworn he heard them pee for almost two minutes straight. He felt a little bad, but he also couldn't help but chuckle a bit.

He made sure that Larry and the random civilian got home safely and then headed straight for Indianapolis. He was sure that his mother would be angry with him when he got there, but he also knew that, deep down, she would understand. She and their father had raised them to be bold, courageous, and loyal, to protect one another at all costs. She couldn't very well be *too* angry; he had no choice regarding how he was brought up.

When he arrived, he walked into the waiting room and was first greeted with a hug from his wife and from his daughter. He could see the relief in his daughter's eyes, and he was glad that she could finally feel at ease. He saw his niece and nephew sitting across the room, and they offered him slight smiles. His brother Mark and parents hugged him next, and his mother sobbed into his shirt.

"It's okay, Mom," he said. "I'm not dead."

He didn't really have much of a way with words, but that was Joe Garrett.

"Marty's in surgery, but they say he's going to be okay," Mendy informed him.

"Joe, what the hell is going on?" Jess jumped in.

She had been standing to the side patiently waiting her turn to talk to her soon-to-be brother-in-law.

"We've had the news on," Cara began, "but they haven't said much."

"That's because nobody knows much," Joe answered. "They still haven't found the guy, and we have no idea why he started shooting."

"When do you think we'll know something?" Jess asked.

Joe shrugged his shoulders.

"It could be morning," he replied. "It's hard telling. My guys will let me know as soon as they know."

It wasn't what anybody wanted to hear, but they had no choice but to accept it and wait. Though the lack of answers gnawed at them, they found peace in the presence of one another. They were a close family, and in times of hardship and pain, nothing provided more solace than being together.

As Joe continued his descent from the high setting of his Warrior Mindset and back down to his normal, daily setting, he wrapped his arm around his wife and leaned back in his seat.

He thought about how proud he was of APD. He thought about how incredible it was to see nurses, police officers, hospital staff, and so many others come together and support his family. And as he looked up at the ceiling, he thanked God for saving his little brother.

Because it was through God that all of this was possible.

Marty had made the right decision to bring Kilo with him into the alley because, if he hadn't, the shooter would have aimed for his head rather than his dog at his feet.

Guthrie had showed up with an AR, without which the shooter may not have run away.

Joe hadn't turned off his radio right after work like he normally would have. If he had turned it off, he wouldn't have known Marty was in trouble.

Joe's truck ended up just feet away from Marty's head, right where it needed to be.

Marty had made the decision to let Larry come with him on a ride-along that night. Without Larry, there would have been nobody to hold the tourniquet.

The firemen made the decision to say screw the rules and "commandeer" the ambulance to save Marty.

And if Joe hadn't been in Fallujah, if he hadn't seen those words written on that porta potty wall, he never would have developed his Warrior Mindset.

None of it was coincidence. Joe didn't believe in coincidence. It was by God's plan, by Divine intervention that his brother was alive. Everything that could've went wrong, went wrong. But everything that could've went right, went right.

And as he looked around the room at his family, he was so thankful for everything that went right.

Chapter 14

Kenneth James Bailey, Jr.

That was the name of the 58-year-old man who opened fire on innocent people on July 26th, 2012 in Pendleton, Indiana. His wife of several years had left him for another man. She filed a restraining order against her soon-to-be ex-husband, and that was the straw that broke the camel's back. Bailey decided that he would get his revenge, and he didn't care who else got hurt in the crossfire.

He parked his car down Water Street a few houses away from her residence and waited for her to get home from work. When she arrived, he parked in the middle of the street in front of her house and grabbed his arsenal. He exited the vehicle and began to call out to her.

He had an AK47 with 200 rounds, a 9mm, a flak jacket, night vision goggles, and a gas mask; it was a ghastly sight. She stared at him in complete fear as he confronted her on the sidewalk, threatening to kill her and then kill himself. She told him that he didn't need to do this, that he couldn't be serious.

At that moment, one of her neighbors, Mr. John Neal Shull, was trying to get home to his wife, but he couldn't get around Bailey's vehicle. Bailey looked at her and said, "Let me show you how serious I am."

He shot seventeen rounds at Mr. Shull's vehicle. Thirteen of the rounds hit him, and he was pronounced dead at the scene. He was only 48 years old.

As Bailey was shooting at Mr. Shull's truck, his wife took off running down the alley that Marty and his fellow officers would venture down later that evening. He tried to shoot her, but his gun jammed. By the time he got it unjammed, she had already found cover. He stood on the sidewalk frustrated, but less than a minute later, two Pendleton police officers arrived on the scene.

He immediately began firing at the vehicle. Thankfully, the only bodily damage that was inflicted was a piece of plastic that broke off of the car door and stuck in one of the officer's legs. The other officer was unharmed.

Kenneth Bailey then took off down the alley to find his estranged wife. It was not long after that that Marty and his fellow officers showed up to assist the fallen police officer. The news of the Pendleton officer's safety had not been relayed to Anderson at that time.

After Joe extracted Marty and returned to the scene, Anderson Police Department still had no knowledge of who the subject was or why he was doing these things. They had been informed by that time that the Pendleton police officer was safe and well, but they still did not know who they were dealing with. They would not find out the whole story until the morning.

While Joe was at the hospital with his family, Anderson officers found the shooter with a self-inflicted gunshot wound to the head. He had hidden behind a house to kill himself, and this made it difficult to locate the body in the dark. He would never get to stand trial for the crimes he committed and the innocent lives he took.

His wife was found taking shelter at a neighbor's house and was unharmed. Though she had called 9-1-1, the news of her safety had not been relayed to Joe while he was searching for the shooter that night.

Though APD and the entire community mourned the loss of Mr. Shull, they were thankful that no other innocent people lost their lives that night. They had done their utmost to protect and to serve. And Kilo, a loyal, brave member of the Anderson Police Department, had given his all. And though Marty missed him terribly, he took comfort in the fact that Kilo would have passed away regardless of whether or not Guthrie took the shot. The shooter had delivered a fatal blow to Kilo's chest from the start, but still he fought on.

Anderson Police Department was the fourth agency on scene that night and the first into the gunfight. A total of 26 APD officers (some in civilian clothes), one county deputy, and two Indiana State Police Troopers made up the perimeter. Most of these men and women were armed only with 9mm handguns, only sixty feet away from a killer who was much better armed and was showing no mercy.

And how did the Garrett and Dulworth families feel about everything that happened that night? After all, feelings are important after a trauma such as this. If you ask any member of the Dulworth or Garrett clan, they will all tell you one thing: they were thankful that this man could no longer harm anyone else. There was no chance of him seeing the light of day again or getting away with the deed on a technicality. There would be no drawn-out court case, no testifying, no reliving the pain of that night in front of a jury. It was over.

Well, the danger was over, anyway. The healing? The getting back to normal?

That was just beginning.

Marty and Kilo at the K9 Olympics in
Peru, IN in 2010

Matt Guthrie's rifle

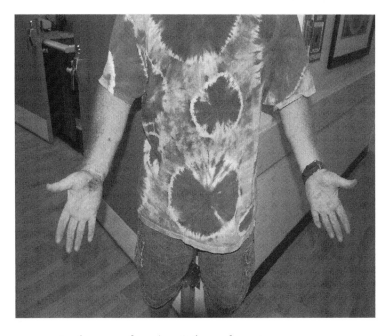

Joe's superhero suit/angel costume

Marty's left boot

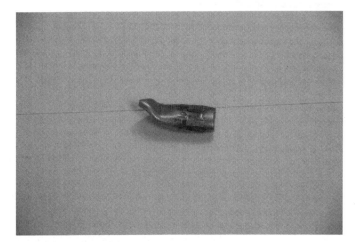

The bullet that hit Marty's left foot

The scene of the crime

Mr. John Neal Shull, the innocent victim

The fierce and loyal Kilo

A photo of Marty shown on several local and national news outlets.

Joe received the Law Enforcement Medal of Valor for his bravery the night of the shooting.

Part 2: A New Kind of Darkness

Chapter 15

A law enforcement family is not like your average family. Sure, every family is different, unique, but law enforcement families have traits that aren't necessarily commonplace. They handle tragedy differently. They know that terrible things could happen to their loved one in law enforcement, but somehow this doesn't shake their faith. They expect the worst, but they hope for the best. They are able to make peace with the fact that anything could happen without sacrificing their sanity.

This mindset, however, doesn't protect them from the consequences of tragedy. They still must deal with them; they still must try to come to terms with the damage that evil can do, what evil did. The Garretts and Dulworths had a lot of emotions to unpack in the days after July 26th, 2012.

Joe's 18-year-old son, Kegan, had stayed home with his younger sisters Sophie and Ava on the night of the shooting. Sophie was just 8 years old and Ava just 6. Though the girls slept through the night, the challenge of explaining what had happened to their uncle rose with the sun the next morning. Kegan had been tasked with making sure that he kept things hidden until his parents returned home. And, when they did return, they had to try to explain the concept of evil to two little girls.

Before this day, the girls were aware that being a police officer was a dangerous job. They would see the news reports of police officers being killed in the line of duty. However, they were consistently reassured by their father that things like that didn't happen in Anderson, it wouldn't happen to their dad or uncle. And now that it had, the girls found themselves confused, sad, and frightened.

They couldn't understand why anyone would want to hurt their uncle. He was one of their best friends, always making time to play with them and make them laugh. Their knowledge of evil before this day was surface-level. Evil was the wicked witch and the malicious queen in their story books or movies. Evil was easy to recognize by a dark cape or a scary cackle. Evil was foreign; it existed in the world, sure, but not in their world. Not in their lives.

Their parents watched over the following weeks as the girls became a little more somber, a little more serious. Though they still played and smiled and carried on, there was a different air about them, a different look in their eyes. Because they were indeed different after that night.

And that is perhaps one of the most disheartening parts of the story. That two little girls had to grow up so quickly, to learn about evil so soon.

If you were to ask Joe Garrett what his greatest regret is about the whole situation, it would be that he didn't prepare his children for that night. He should have been honest with them about the dangers of his job, of their uncle's job. He should have done all he could to make sure that if the day ever came when he or their uncle got injured or didn't come home at all, they would be ready. He didn't, though, and he felt that he had failed them because of this.

If you were to ask Irene Dulworth how she felt regarding that night, regarding the shooter, she would say that one must follow the Christian path of forgiveness. She would also tell you that it's important to pray for the shooter's family because, although his actions were despicable, it isn't the fault of his family, and they deserve comfort, as well. The size of her heart makes her a forgiving woman, but it also makes her a sensitive one.

She always worried about Joe and Marty, even before that summer night. But now, one mention of that night sends her into a fit of tears. She worries constantly, because she now knows that terrible things can happen to any family. It happened to her family.

If you were to ask Joe, he would tell you that he doesn't spare a thought for his brother's shooter. He cannot justify letting the man rent space in his head, and he doesn't. It is not a part of the Warrior Mindset. It has changed his life, certainly, but he will not allow the man to change his Warrior Mindset, to make him stop doing what he is called to do.

Kegan and Cara were old enough at the time to know that evil existed, but this didn't make things any easier for them. Like their cousins Ryan and Hayley, they were at an age where peer scrutiny was an unavoidable consequence of such a chaotic event. It would grow annoying to them, to constantly answer questions and be the center of attention, but they all tried to remember that things would eventually return to normal.

The hardest part for all four of them, though, was dealing with their new reality. Not the reality that their family was the talk of the town or that Marty now had a lifelong injury or that Kilo was gone, but the reality that their dad and their uncle aren't bulletproof. They used to say goodbye to them when they went to work without questioning whether or not they would come back; they no longer had that luxury. The thought of each goodbye being their final one always creeps in. And although they were raised to be strong, and although they are always skilled enough to push the thought away and carry on with their days, it was a new reality that was difficult to adjust to.

Mendy struggled following the shooting. She was arguably the strongest family member at the hospital that night, but her strength crumbled the moment she gave it permission to do so. It was a lot to ask of someone, after all, to hold it together on a night of so much tragedy, but her strength was the glue that held the family together that night.

She knew what kind of man Joe was when she married him: a warrior who runs toward the fight, not away from it. This was the kind of life she knew she may have. She knew that a night such as that one was a possibility. She also knew that without God, and without prayer, things would not have turned out as well as they did.

The days following the shooting would affect every member of the Dulworth family. They would all have to adjust to their new reality. They would all worry more, but they would also love more. They would grow in their faith. They would grow closer together. They would look to God for their strength from above and to one another for their strength on Earth.

Things would never be the same; they all knew this. But, that didn't mean that things would never be good again. Who knew? Maybe with a little help from above, some things would somehow be even better than before.

Chapter 16

If you were to ask Marty Dulworth about the days following the shooting, his answer would be quick and concise: "I don't remember". The pain that he was in would have been intolerable without pain medication. A simple gunshot wound to the foot would have been a little easier to recover from, but this wound wasn't at all simple. A majority of his foot was gone, left in a scattered mess in the alley where it had to be cleaned up after the chaos had subsided.

The surgery he had the night of the shooting was for one purpose: control the bleeding and prevent infection. They repaired what damage they could to make sure that Marty was stable and packed the wound with antibiotics. That wouldn't be enough to send him home, though. Only one of the arteries that went down the front of his foot was able to be repaired. The time came, then, to decide how best to repair what was left, and how to replace what was gone.

The first few surgeries were simply focused on packing the wound, encouraging tissue regrowth, and reattaching and mending what they could. This had to be done over the course of several days so as to not overwhelm Marty's fragile body.

After these surgeries were finished, the cosmetic surgeon had to come up with a way to replace the lost muscles and tendons in the foot. The foot needed a muscular foundation if Marty were to ever bear weight on it again. The orthopedic surgeon and cosmetic surgeon teamed up to fix this problem. In a 12-hour-long procedure, the orthopedic surgeon placed wires and bolts into the foot to create a metal base, and the cosmetic surgeon removed a piece of muscle from Marty's abdomen and grafted it onto the foot.

It was rudimentary at best. This wasn't due to a lack of skill from the doctors, but it was simply how the cookie crumbled. Science is, of course, incredible, but there's only so much it can do at this point in human history. It didn't look like a foot, but it would eventually be able to hold Marty up. After the surgery, he wore a size 11 shoe on his right foot and a 14 wide on his left. It wasn't a beautiful foot, but it was a foot.

Sort of.

And if you ask Marty how he felt between all of these surgeries, or if he was worried or afraid, or who all visited him, his answer would still be: "I don't remember". If you've ever had a crazy night with too much alcohol, reader, and woken up the next day with pieces of your night missing, gone forever, try to harness that feeling. Try to remember the frustration you felt as you tried to remember the jokes and the tomfoolery and the conversation.

Now, imagine that you're trying to remember some of the most defining days of your life. You're trying to remember the heartfelt words and thanks from families and friends. You try and try to recover a snippet of a conversation, an image of a face, but you can't. That was what the pain medication did to Marty.

Most of the days in the hospital were the same. He either was in surgery, getting prepped for a surgery, seeing visitors, or sleeping. There was one day, however, that was different from the rest, one day that was special. This day, though he can barely remember it, was one of the best days of his life.

Saturday August 11th, 2012. That was the day that Marty and Jess were supposed to be married. The invitations had been sent, the dress had been bought, and everything had been planned. But, as they had learned, life doesn't always go according to plan. And, as they had also learned, nobody is guaranteed tomorrow.

Likewise, nobody is guaranteed a partner to love, a person to spend the rest of their life with. Marty's family could see how much Jess cared for Marty, how much she loved him. She was as loyal as any woman you could find on this Earth, and everyone knew it.

Jess and Marty were devastated that they weren't going to get the wedding that they had planned, but then they thought, "So what if *that* wedding was off?" It didn't mean that they couldn't schedule a new one.

The couple decided that the shooter had already taken so much from them; he didn't get to take anything else. They wouldn't let him. They were going to get married on August 11th, 2012 even if they had to do it right there in the hospital room.

As anyone who works in a hospital will know, it doesn't take long for word to spread on a nursing floor. When one of the nurses overheard them discussing plans to bring their pastor in so they could say their vows, she decided that this couple needed to have more than just a simple vow exchange. The nurses banded together to buy decorations and food and planned a reception in the waiting room. One of the nurse's mom actually owned a baking business and donated a gorgeous wedding cake for the big day. Jess' friends brought her dress to her and did her hair and makeup for the ceremony.

And although it wasn't exactly everything they had imagined their wedding day to be, it was beautiful. One of the strongest vows in existence is the vow between a police officer and their spouse. Jess knew that being married to a police officer would always be a challenge, but she hadn't expected all of this. She hadn't expected such an overwhelming challenge right off the bat.

It would have been easy for Jess to run away. The future was uncertain, after all. There was a possibility that Marty would one day have to have his leg amputated. There was a possibility that he wouldn't be able to go back to work. There was a possibility that she would have to care for him for the rest of their lives.

But she made her vow to him anyway. And that is the heart of loyalty, the heart of marriage.

For better or for worse.

For richer or for poorer.

In sickness and in health.

Chapter 17

All in all, Marty was in the hospital for three weeks before he was finally allowed to go home, and he was so happy. He just wanted to sleep in his own bed, to be in Middletown and to have the windows open and hear the birds chirping, to be close to his family again. He was still in immense pain, but at least he was in immense pain in the comfort of his own home.

And he was married now. He could barely remember the ceremony, but he knew that he was definitely married. He wished that they were spending their first day in their home as a married couple under different circumstances, but that was okay. He was just happy that he could now call Jess his wife.

Though he was allowed to go home, the pain medication was still a necessity; dealing with the pain would be a long battle. However, taking the medication by mouth instead of by IV made things a little easier, made his mind less groggy. The side effects didn't go away entirely, but it was manageable for the time being. And he had Jess to care for him; she had taken time off work to be by his side.

Though Marty knew he would be stuck in his house for several months, he was uplifted by the constant stream of visitors. Every day brought a visitor, and most days brought a food dish of some kind. People told him that he was a hero, they applauded him for his bravery, but that wasn't what kept his spirits up. He just enjoyed the company. He just enjoyed being around people who made him smile, who made him forget, if only temporarily, about the trauma and the pain. He needed these people; he needed them to protect him from the darkness that lingered on the borders of his mind.

He had to keep it at bay.

Jess, however, didn't enjoy the visitors as much as Marty. She was grateful to them for visiting and for caring about Marty, she truly was. But, being a caregiver is not an easy job. It is physically and emotionally draining. It can make you want to get away from any and all people.

Not forever, just for a while.

She wanted to tell Marty that the visitors had to stop for a while, even just at least a few hours in the day when nobody was there. She just wanted her house back. She just wanted to be alone with her husband. Life was not going according to plan, and she had made peace with that, but it didn't make the constant chaos any less overwhelming.

However, she took comfort in the fact that the visitors would eventually stop coming, and then she would get some well-earned quiet time. But, she wondered, how would Marty feel then?

Though Jess wondered about this, Joe knew the answer well. And he knew that Marty needed to know the answer, though he had never asked the question.

Joe had been over to check on Marty every day for the two weeks he had been home. Everyone in their family had been over nearly every day. Marty and Hayley's relationship was on the mend; she came over and read the Bible to him every evening. Their parents stopped in and checked on him after work. He always had somebody, always.

This day when Joe stopped in, he knew he was going to have to make his brother upset. He hoped, though, that this little dose of truth would save him more hurt in the long run.

"Hey, Joe!"

Marty was lounging on the couch watching a movie when Joe walked through the front door.

"Hey, man," Joe replied as he plopped down on the couch next to him. "How ya feelin'?"

"Oh, about the same," he answered. "I had a few visitors today so that was nice. And check out all of this!"

Marty and Jess had been receiving cards and donations from people all over the country; their haul on that day was quite impressive. From police departments to Sunday school classes, people showered them with love, encouragement, and thanks. It was overwhelming, and it lit up those dark days.

The Anderson K9 Department had received cards and donations, as well. Just weeks after Kilo's murder, another police canine, Magnum, was killed in the line of duty. Kilo's and Magnum's memorial service had taken place the day before. It was a beautiful service attended by hundreds of locals and dozens of K9 handlers from all over the country, from California to North Dakota to Florida. Though it was heartbreaking to say goodbye to his partner, he felt relieved that he was now laid to rest with all the honors he deserved. Robert Loose Funeral Home had kept his body until the service, and they respected the family's wishes and their mourning just as they would if the deceased had been human.

"I can't believe all of this," Marty added with a grin. "This support is amazing."

Joe nodded his head and grinned slightly.

"Listen, Marty, you might think about preparing yourself for when the cards and visitors stop coming."

Marty cast him a confused glance as he rearranged himself on the cushion.

"You've been through hell these past weeks, but you've always had people around. Tons of people. But as much as all these people love you, they're going to stop visiting. Life is going to slow down and things are going to have to start getting back to normal. That's when the real recovery is going to start."

His little brother didn't respond right away. He stared at the floor, and Joe realized that Marty likely hadn't thought about this at all before this moment.

"Yeah, you're right," Marty replied. "I know you're right. I'll be okay."

Joe nodded his head again. He knew that his brother would be okay eventually, but he knew that it would be a struggle. It would be a struggle for him and Jess both. But they would make it through; he had no doubts.

"I know you will," Joe said. "You're a Dulworth. We were raised to be okay, to make it through."

He grabbed his brother's shoulder and gave it a little shake.

"Right," Marty whispered. "I'll be okay."

Chapter 18

The darkness had been waiting for weeks to make its move. It lingered in the back of Marty's mind, building and gathering strength for its first attack. The light that came from the love and company of Marty's visitors had held it back for a while, but that worked out well for the darkness. It gave it time to prepare.

The pain meds fueled the darkness, too, though Jess had weaned him off of most of them. He was only on hydrocodone, but that was enough for the darkness. It changed Marty's personality, made him snippy, moody, and downright mean at times. The darkness fed on this negativity; it loved it. It watched as the days passed by and the visitors became few and far between until, eventually, they stopped altogether. The only people that stopped by were Marty's family, and even they had to get back to their normal routines.

This darkness was one that Marty had only toed the line with before. He remembered the darkness he had felt when he was going through his divorce, when he was drinking and partying, when he got his DUI. He remembered the darkness when he was suspended, when he felt shame for what he had done. That darkness had convinced him that he was a disgrace, that he was past the point of no return, that his reputation was ruined and that he should leave it where it lie.

This new darkness, though, was darker even than that.

This kind of darkness didn't attack like other kinds. Real darkness occludes the vision, it incites fear. It comes on suddenly, like when you flip off a light or take the first step into the unlit alley. This darkness, though, this darkness was cruel and slow and unforgiving. It didn't hit him all at once. It crept in.

It started its assault by making him mean. He loved Jess so much, but he couldn't help but be mean sometimes. His hateful remarks, his bad attitude when she was just trying to help.

Then it crept into his physical being. It seemed that the more the darkness crept in, the more pain he felt. And he felt pain in new places, headaches and nausea. It felt like his body was falling apart, that it would never recover from this trauma.

Then it slipped into his mind, into his sleep. The nightmares were unrelenting. He would wake up in the middle of the night screaming, waking

Jess and the kids if they were staying over. That night replayed over and over again in his mind, each time convincing him that he would never get to see his family again, that it was all over. And when he would wake up screaming, lying in a puddle of sweat, he would realize that although he was alive, he still wasn't out of the woods. Not yet.

The darkness turned him into a zombie, a shell of who he had been before. It crept into his skin, his bones, his soul. And it didn't just affect him.

Jess was with him all the time, every day. The darkness crept into the atmosphere, and it eventually crept into her mind. She thought about how things were supposed to be, how the first weeks of their married life should be. She began to worry about the future.

"What if I have to take care of him for the rest of our lives?"

"What if he doesn't get better?"

"What if he can never go back to work?"

These thoughts never made a home in her mind, though. They sometimes were able to set up a temporary camp, but they were always quickly expelled.

"In sickness and in health."

That was her vow, and she had meant it. She loved him, and she had faith that this darkness would soon be chased away. It would not live in their home forever.

It would not live in Marty's mind forever.

This, all of this, is what Joe had been referring to, but Marty hadn't realized just how powerful this new darkness would be. He hadn't realized that every day would be a struggle while this darkness ruled over him.

But, that's the way with this kind of darkness.

That's the way with depression.

There were two things that prevented Marty's downfall, his complete surrender to this darkness. The first was the way that he was raised. He was a Dulworth. His father grew up in the heart of the Great Depression, a time when if you didn't push through, you didn't make it. His parents expected strength and perseverance from him and his brothers. They weren't allowed to quit. It wasn't an option.

The second was his family. They tried to visit every day, but they had other responsibilities, as well, other places to be. He understood this. And Jess was always there. As mean as he was to her at times because of the pain medications and the darkness, as stressful as things got, she was there. If it weren't for Jess and the rest of his family, if it weren't for their love, the darkness would have won.

The dark days seemed like they would last forever, like a rainstorm that's taking its own sweet time passing over. The thing about rainstorms is that, before the invention of weather surveillance radar, nobody knew how long they would last. Now, we have the luxury of turning on one of the several weather channels and looking at an easy-to-read, color-coded picture that tells us how heavy the rain will be, where it will fall, and how long before the sunshine returns.

Marty didn't have this luxury. He knew that the storm would pass, but he had no idea when. After weeks of suffering through the downpour, he started to grow accustomed to it. It became a temporary normal. However, all storms must come to an end eventually.

One morning in October, Marty woke up to the sunlight pouring in through his window. He had woken up on many sunny mornings, but this one was different. The sunshine seemed to penetrate his skin and touch his soul. He felt warm. Not hot or sweaty like he felt after his nightmares, but warm and comforted and safe.

He heard the birds chirping outside the window. He was sure that the birds had probably chirped every morning since the shooting, but he hadn't heard them until this day. Their song had no words, but it somehow still told him that all was well.

And just like that, the rainstorm was over. The darkness had been defeated. It hadn't been a grand battle; it had simply been the clouds passing over, the downpour turning into a sprinkle, and the sun taking its rightful spot once more.

He couldn't help but chuckle a bit. He hadn't expected the darkness to be defeated in this way, but he would take it. Perhaps, he thought, it was a God thing. So often, God is battling for us, right by our side, and we don't even notice. Marty noticed, though.

He sat up in bed and looked at Jess sleeping soundly next to him, her dark hair covering half of her face. He decided then and there that he wasn't going to let the darkness take hold again. It would creep in from time to time, no doubt, but it would never again sit on the throne. The sunshine was back, and Marty wasn't about to let it get away.

Not today.

Chapter 19

Marty was trying to be optimistic as he put on his uniform on that bitterly cold January night. He knew that he should be grateful that he was going back to work, but he wished he was hoping back in the car with Kilo. His heart sank as he thought about his fallen partner, but he knew that he couldn't dwell on it. He had to get going.

Sitting at the desk couldn't be too bad, right? He'd done it before here and there, but he avoided it whenever possible. Anything had to be better than sitting on the couch. Anything had to be better than watching more sitcom reruns and sleeping for twelve hours a day. At least he got to put the uniform on again. And anyway, the desk job thing was only for a few months. It would be fine.

Right?

He slipped on his specially-made shoes: 14 wide on the left, 11 on the right. His foot still hurt when he had to bear weight on it, but it would get better. With enough physical therapy and time to heal, he would be back to his old self in no time. So what if he had to wear a giant shoe? It was a small price to pay for the freedom of getting back out on the streets doing what he loved: protecting and serving.

He looked at his watch. He would probably arrive at the station early, but that was just fine with him. Some extra time for adjustment would be good; he would probably need a refresher.

As he walked out the front door, the freezing air stole the breath from his lungs. He thought about winter nights driving around the city with Kilo, trying to stay warm but knowing that Indiana winters are even more brutal than Indiana summers. You could bundle up, turn the heat on in your car, but the cold would still win in the end.

He slowly walked to his car.

"Take it slow," he thought to himself. "Remember what the doctor said. Take it slow."

Though taking it slow was frustrating for a man who was constantly on the move, he knew that this was the intelligent choice. His foot was healing, but it still needed to be babied for a while longer. He was to be resting it as much as possible so that when the time came for him to take his fitness test to get back in the field, he would be ready.

Another reason he had to take it slow was because the ground was covered in snow and ice. He managed to make it to the car without slipping and falling, but the roads were sure to be terrible. That was the price he paid for the solace of living in a rural area.

As he pulled out of the driveway, he felt as though he was in a dream. It didn't seem real. After five months of surgeries and physical therapy and days sitting in a fog of medication and depression, he was finally going back to work. He had to be on time somewhere besides a doctor appointment!

He drove slowly down the road admiring the stars shining through the bare trees. Bare of leaves, anyway; they were shimmering in the moonlight from the ice and snow that adorned their branches. He realized then that he had never paid attention to things like that before.

Nearly dying changes a person in many ways, and one of those ways is that you notice things. You don't just notice things in nature, but you also notice things in others and in yourself. Marty had begun to notice how Jess looked so content and beautiful as she got ready for work in the morning. He noticed how his little nieces' eyes lit up whenever they got to visit him. He noticed how Ryan was starting to look more like a man than a boy and how Hayley was growing more and more mature with each passing day. He noticed how much his parents loved each other; he could see it in everything they did now. All of these things had been hidden from him before. Or, rather, he hadn't thought to look for them before.

But he didn't have to even think now; it was automatic. These things jumped out at him like a splash of color in a world of gray. That's what nearly dying does to you, really; it makes you see color in places where you used to see nothing at all.

When he reached the station, he sat in his car for a moment and pulled out his phone to call Jess; he had promised her he would call when he had arrived safely. Jess had been back to work for two months already, and they were both glad that Marty was back to work so that maybe, hopefully, things could start getting back to normal.

After he said goodbye, he walked in the door and was greeted by a fellow officer.

"Hey Marty," he said as he reached out to shake his hand. "How ya feelin'?

"Much better," Marty answered. "Thanks. Ready to get back to it."

"I bet!"

The two men headed to roll call. Everyone was happy to see Marty, and he was happy to see them. Though he wished he was going out into the field, he reminded himself once again that desk duty was better than couch duty.

After roll call, he took his spot behind the desk. The police station was a barren place at 10:00 at night; Marty hated the emptiness. His job was simple: run the station and make sure nobody came in or out who wasn't supposed to.

As he sat listening to the radio at the desk, he felt the darkness start to creep in once again. While everyone else was out on the streets, he was stuck sitting in a chair. With every call that went out, the darkness grew, and the pain increased. Each sound seemed to stab his wounds, reminding him of his current state.

"This is better than being at home," he reminded himself. "At least I'm in my uniform. At least I'm making money."

But the more he told himself these things, the less he believed them. And over the next two months as he sat behind that desk, it took all of his strength to keep the darkness at bay.

Chapter 20

The day had finally arrived. Marty practically jumped out of bed that bitter February morning and put on his athletic gear. Today was the day that he took the physical fitness test that would get him off of desk duty and back out into the field.

He was beyond ready to get back out there. He hated that desk more than anything. He wanted to chop it with an axe, light it on fire, and watch it turn to ashes in front of him. He couldn't stand one more day behind that desk, so he had to pass this test.

He had to be at the testing facility in Indianapolis by 8am. The test would take a little over two hours, and then he would know if his suffering at the desk was over. He was anxious as he drove down the interstate.

He knew what to expect, though. He had been practicing for the test for weeks. He would have to push a weighted sled for 100 meters, run up and down a flight of steps, simulate getting in and out of a police car, and jog on treadmill for 400 meters. And he didn't have to do this only once, but over and over and over again for two hours.

His foot wasn't exactly in tip-top shape; he knew this and Jess knew this. Though the pain wasn't as bad as it had been right after the surgeries, it still hurt. It would never feel normal again according to the doctor, but Marty didn't care. If it could get him from place to place, if it could pass this test, he would take it.

When he arrived at the facility, he signed in and warmed up a bit. He looked down at his enormous left shoe and sighed. He felt a little doubt begin to creep in as he thought about how disadvantaged this giant lump of meat left him, but he didn't let it overtake him.

He thought about his conversation with Joe the day before.

"You know, Marty, some people at the ER asked me if I was impressed that you were going to get back into the field."

"Oh yeah? What'd you tell them?"

"Asked them why I should be impressed. You're a Dulworth. We were raised by the same parents. We aren't allowed to quit. We can't quit. It's not in our nature. I'm not gonna be impressed at you doing something you should be doing in the first place."

Marty wasn't surprised by his brother's answer. He chuckled at the thought of it.

"I can do this," he whispered. "I'm a Dulworth. I can do this."

He approached the starting line when his name was called. He took in a deep breath and freed his mind of any distractions. He was not going to fail.

Not today.

And when the whistle blew, he proved it. For two hours he pushed through the pain. Though he wasn't as fast or as coordinated as he would have been before his injury, he succeeded. He surprised every single person there as he accomplished every single task set before him. And at the end of the two hours, he got the piece of paper. This one little piece of paper that gave him his freedom back.

The piece of paper that he would take to his supervisor and say, "Put me back in the field."

He was glad that he wouldn't have to attack the desk. He was glad that the darkness wouldn't have an easy way back in. And although he knew that overcoming these obstacles was expected of him (by his family and by himself), he allowed himself to feel a little proud of himself.

But as he walked back to his car, as the high from the test wore off, he felt a pain so excruciating that it took him back to the night of the shooting. He sat down in his car, scooted his seat back, and took off his boot. He was worried about what he would find, but the foot looked the same as it always had.

"Maybe I just overdid it today," Marty thought. "I'll ice it and rest it and it'll be better soon."

This is what he told himself as he drove home in agonizing pain. Over the next several days, this reassurance began to fade, and eventually he could no longer convince himself of its truth. He had messed something up, and he had messed it up good.

But he was getting back into the field. Nothing was going to stop him. He would ice it every night, take anti inflammatories every day, and try to avoid extra physical activity outside of work. He would do whatever it took.

He had freed himself from that damn desk, and he was *not* going back.

Chapter 21

Marty's first night back on patrol duty felt like being resurrected from the dead. This new life gave him an ethereal glow and a smile that was contagious, even to a bunch of serious police officers at roll call. Everyone was happy for him, and everyone was glad to have him back.

It would be a while before Marty would be well enough to get back on K9 duty. They would have to purchase a new canine, for one, and for two, Marty would have to be strong enough and well enough to train and handle a new dog. Though Marty felt that he was ready to jump right back into his K9 duties, both his Chief and his doctor recommended that he take things slowly.

It was frustrating. He had been taking things slowly for seven months. He was sick of it. However, as he walked to his car after roll call, he remembered to count his blessings. He was back in the field, and he was grateful. He sat in the driver's seat and looked out the window at the stars.

"Thanks," he said.

He had been praying a lot lately, asking for things and saying thank you for things. But tonight, he wouldn't ask for anything. He would just give thanks. Things were finally starting to work out. He was on the upswing, and he had God to thank for it.

As he drove through Anderson's downtown, all of those old feelings began to flood back. The rush of chasing down a criminal, the thrill of catching him and starting the process of justice. The boring feelings came back, too, like the mundaneness of issuing a speeding ticket, but even for that he was thankful. Those feelings fought off the darkness and lit up his nights.

He missed Kilo, though. He missed him so much. It wasn't the same without him; it never would be. It felt strange being alone in the car, but as the months passed along, he grew used to it. He didn't like it, but he grew used to it. After all, what's one more change in this year of chaos?

And, after all, he was never alone for long. He couldn't pull a person over for a broken headlight without another Anderson officer showing up. He knew why they did it. They were all police brothers and sisters, after all. They had each other's back always. He appreciated it, but as winter and spring passed and summer came along again, he wished they would cut back just a bit.

He was venting to Jess about this one August morning as he sat on the couch struggling to take his left boot off.

"I know they mean well," he said, "but I can handle these things on my own now. It's been over a year since the shooting and I've been back in the field for six months."

He groaned as he finally slipped the boot off. Jess offered him a half smile as she sat on the ottoman in front of him.

"Put your foot up here," she said as she patted her lap.

"It's fine," he argued.

"Let me see it."

He sighed. There was no point in arguing.

He placed his foot in her lap and she placed her thumbs where his foot met his ankle.

"Ready?" she asked.

He nodded his head.

She dug her thumbs into the muscle and pulled his foot toward her. Marty groaned as he felt the pressure in the area release. When they had first figured out this trick, Jess would wince at the pops and cracks, but it was normal now. She was essentially separating his foot from his tibia and fibula, but it was the only way to relieve the pressure and some of the pain.

"Better?" she asked.

"Yeah," he replied. "A little. Thanks, babe."

She nodded her head as she rubbed his leg.

"Is it getting any better day to day?"

He didn't answer her right away. He wanted to tell her that it was getting better, or even that it was staying the same, but both were lies.

"No. No, in fact, I think it's getting worse."

She moved his foot from her lap on to the ottoman and sat next to him on the couch. He wrapped his arm around her, and they sat in silence for a few minutes. They had both been thinking the same thing for weeks now, but neither of them wanted to say it. They had spent so long trying to avoid it, but maybe it was time to consider it.

"I've, uh, I've been thinking about what the doctor said," Marty whispered. "What he said about amputation."

He expected Jess to free herself from his arm and stare at him with wild eyes, but she didn't budge. Amputation had always been an option, but Marty wanted so badly to avoid it. He would try anything. But always, at every appointment, his doctor reminded him of the option. If the pain ever got too bad, if the struggle became too great, the option was there.

"Have you?" Jess asked.

"Yeah. The pain is just…"

He paused. He felt weak even admitting it, but he knew that it was true. The pain was becoming unbearable. Like he said, it had been over a year since the shooting, and still the pain wasn't gone. His foot barely functioned. Things weren't getting better.

"I think it's time," Jess agreed.

He was surprised at the surety in her voice.

"Yeah?" he asked.

"Babe, you can't take a step without feeling like someone is stabbing your foot. You have trouble sleeping because of the pain. I just wonder if, maybe, amputation might solve a lot of your problems."

"But it could cause problems too, Jess. I could be stuck in a wheelchair."

"You won't be stuck in a wheelchair," she assured him. "They have prosthetic legs."

He cringed at that word: *prosthetic*. He didn't want to have to wear a prosthetic. He didn't want to not be able to do the things he wanted to do.

But then he realized that, actually, he already couldn't do a lot of the things he wanted to do.

"It's terrifying," he admitted. "I'll literally be losing half a limb."

"I know. But really Marty, you kind of already have. At least with a prosthetic maybe you could do things without pain. It'd take some getting used to, but if anybody can do it, it's you."

He didn't reply, and he felt her snuggle up closer to him. Before long though, her phone began to ring from her pocket.

"Just think on it, babe," Jess said as she stood up. "Your appointment isn't for another week. You've got time. And you know that I support you, whatever you decide."

He grabbed her hand as she started to walk away and pulled her back toward him. And as he kissed her, the two of them smiled.

"I know you will. Thank you."

And although he had plenty of time to think on it, as he watched her walk toward the bedroom to take her call, he had already made up his mind. He wasn't going to live his life in pain any longer. He was going to find a way to do all the things he used to do. If it meant amputation, if it meant wearing a prosthetic, so be it. He would find a way.

He would do it for his family.

Kilo & Magnum's Memorial Service

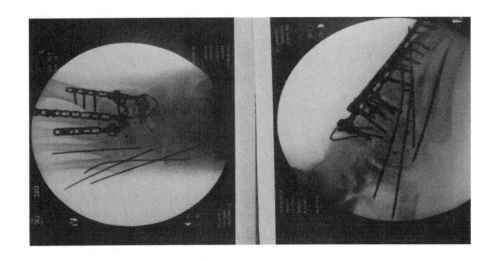

Marty's new foot

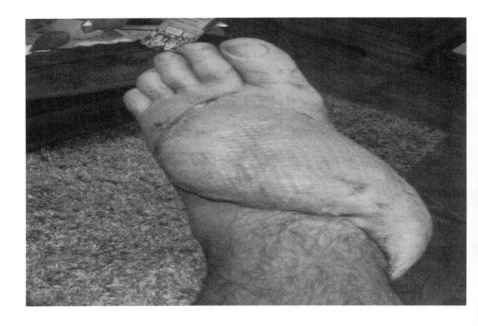

Part 3: Reaching for the Light

Chapter 22

It was a typical Indiana August day when Marty and Jess drove to Indy for his appointment with his orthopedic surgeon. The heat and humidity took him back to the day of the shooting, the day when it all started. He thought about that day as Jess took the exit toward the orthopedic center.

When they reached the parking lot, Marty felt the nagging doubts begin to creep into his mind.

What if you can't walk right on a prosthetic?

What if you can't get around any better?

What if the pain from the amputation is worse than your pain now?

He felt the doubts flee, though, as Jess touched his arm.

"Ready?" she asked.

He nodded his head.

"Ready," he replied.

They got out of the car and headed into the building. When they walked into the waiting room, a woman with a clipboard was waiting for them. They knew her well by this point, and they greeted her with a smile. She was a representative from the City of Anderson's workers compensation company, and she had been at every single one of Marty's surgeries and appointments.

Though at first it was irritating to have her around, they understood that she was just doing her job, and they actually grew to like her. She was friendly and caring, and though she was paid to act in the company's best interest, they felt that she still cared about them. They felt that she still acted ethically and respectably.

They waited for only a couple of minutes after checking in before a medical assistant called them back to the exam room. The workers compensation woman waited outside the room as Marty got changed, and when Jess opened the door after he was finished, both she and the doctor walked in.

"Hi there. How are we feeling?" the doctor asked.

"Oh, I've felt better," Marty replied with a chuckle.

"Well, let's take a look at that foot, shall we?"

The doctor extended the end of the patient bed so Marty could stretch out his leg. And as he examined the foot, the doctor began to realize that many things were off.

"Has it been painful?" he asked.

"Incredibly," Marty answered.

He looked to Jess who nodded at him to continue.

"Actually, it's been getting worse and worse every day," Marty continued.

"Well, you've probably torn some things in here with all your activity on the job," the doctor said as he pushed on different spots of the foot. "We'll have to do surgery to fix the spots and-"

"Actually, doc, I was thinking…"

The doctor stopped poking the foot and looked up at him. Marty cleared his throat.

"I was thinking that I don't wanna deal with another surgery. It's too painful. I think I wanna take you up on your original offer from last year."

Marty thought that the doctor would try to talk him out of it, so he had prepared his reasoning, his arguments. But, he was shocked when he saw a smile emerge on the man's face.

"Yeah, I wondered how long it would take you," he replied.

"Really?" Marty asked.

"Really," he answered with a chuckle. "You fought longer than anyone else would have. And hey, don't think of this as giving up. You're not giving up, you're just taking the next logical step. You'll see."

Jess grabbed Marty's hand, and they both smiled at one another. The workers compensation woman even managed a smile as she quickly jotted down notes.

"So, it's an inpatient procedure. The surgery itself will only take about an hour, but we'll want to monitor you for a couple of days to watch for signs of infection. Overall, though, it'll be pretty painless. The ladies out front will get it scheduled for you. Also, they'll get you set up with SRT Prosthetics. They'll send a representative out to your place to talk to you about the process and how to adjust to living with a prosthetic limb."

"Okay. Sounds good," Marty replied.

"Any questions?"

"Um, no, not at the moment. Jess?"

She shook her head.

"Well, you just give the office a call if you think of any," he said as he washed his hands. "We'll be happy to answer them for you. And, of course, we'll be in contact with you with your pre-procedure instructions and such. Okay?"

Marty and Jess nodded. The workers compensation woman finally set her pencil down, and she nodded, as well.

"Great. You folks take care."

And just like that, it was decided. It happened so quickly. In just a three-minute conversation, Marty had decided to let a doctor cut off half of his leg.

"You okay?" Jess asked.

"Yeah, let's go get this thing scheduled," he said as he stepped down from the bed.

The drive home was eerily quiet. The reality of his situation was starting to sink in. It felt different now that he had finally decided to do it, now that he had it scheduled. He felt the darkness begin to amass in the far corners of his mind.

"You made the right decision, babe," Jess said.

He didn't respond. He just stared out the window at the cars zooming past them on the interstate.

It didn't seem real. After all the surgeries, all the physical therapy, all the struggle, he was getting his leg cut off. It seemed like it had all been for nothing.

Jess was probably right, though. And it was like the doctor had said, it was the next logical step.

Ugh, *step*. He hated that word. He hated it because all it brought to mind was a terrifying question:

What would his steps be like after this amputation?

Chapter 23

Less than a week after the appointment with his orthopedic doctor, Marty sat on his front porch waiting for the SRT Prosthetics representative to show up for their meeting. Marty wasn't exactly sure what to expect, but he knew that it would be a casual meeting. He had cleaned up the living room and made some iced tea for the occasion, but that was about it. He was wondering whether or not he should grab a journal to take notes when a car pulled into the driveway.

Out of the car stepped a lanky, curly haired, bearded man in a v-neck t-shirt and jeans. He looked like he was barely out of high school. Marty could feel the irritation begin to grow.

"This company really sent some college-aged intern who's just trying to make enough money over the summer so he can go screw around in Cancun on fall break," he thought.

The man waved and smiled, and Marty returned the gestures despite his overwhelming annoyance.

"Marty?" the man asked as he stuck out his hand.

"Yes, hello," Marty replied as he stood and shook his hand.

"My name's Ashton from SRT Prosthetics. It's a pleasure to meet you. Do you want to talk out here?"

"Nah, it's hot as hell out here. We can go inside and sit on the couch."

Marty opened the front door and gestured inside. Ashton sat on the couch and stretched out his right leg beside the ottoman.

"Uh, I made some iced tea. Would you like some?" Marty asked.

"That'd be great, thanks," he answered.

Marty headed into the kitchen to pour a glass. This kid's over-the-top cheeriness was starting to wear on his nerves. When he returned to the living room, he saw that he had placed a couple brochures out on the ottoman. Marty set the glass of tea on the end table for him.

"Thanks!" Ashton chirped. "So, your surgery is in two weeks?"

"Yeah," Marty answered.

"How are you feeling?"

Marty wanted to roll his eyes. What did this kid care? He just wanted to make a sale, and he'd do it regardless of how Marty felt about his procedure.

"Well, it's not an ideal situation, but it is what it is. I'm hoping there'll be more positives than negatives from it."

"Yeah, I get that. I was more nervous than anything. I didn't know what life would be like as an amputee."

And just as he finished his sentence, he rolled his pants leg up to reveal a prosthetic leg.

"Wait, you're an amputee?" Marty asked, not at all attempting to mask the shock in his voice.

Ashton chuckled.

"Yeah, it's kind of one of the major qualifications for this job," he replied.

Marty chuckled in return and, in truth, he began to feel a little guilty for all of his false assumptions about the kid.

"So, I'm here to answer any questions you've got about life with a prosthetic leg. I can either start by giving kind of a summary of things, or if you have any specific questions we can start there."

Marty had a hundred questions, but there was one that had been burning in his mind since the moment he had made the decision to amputate.

"So, what kinds of things can you not do anymore because you have a prosthetic?"

Ashton shrugged his shoulders and smiled.

"I can pretty much do whatever I want. It's different, yeah, but it doesn't stop me from doing the things I want to do. Prosthetics are incredible. They enable people to do more than they ever thought possible post-amputation."

Marty nodded his head. He didn't know what to say. All of the doubts and worries that had been swimming through his mind were suddenly disproven and cast aside.

"Let me prove it to you," Ashton added. "Are you free Wednesday afternoon?"

***

On Wednesday afternoon, Ashton picked Marty up from his house and the two headed to the city of Muncie just north of Middletown. They were going to an event that brought together amputees from across the country to showcase just how normal life can be with a prosthetic. When they arrived, Marty was blown away by what he saw.

There were dozens of amputees, and they all walked like Ashton. They all walked perfectly normally. In fact, it was Marty and the people like him who walked terribly.

Everyone was either an amputee or a person who would soon be an amputee. Marty got to talk to people who were going through the same struggles as he was. He got to talk to amputees who showed him the exercises they do to keep up their strength. They showed him how they learned to walk again, and they shared with him everything they went through.

It wasn't going to be easy; Marty knew this. And that's what these people told him. It wouldn't be easy, but it would be worth it. He got phone numbers from people all over the country who told him to call or text them with any questions, or if he just needed to talk through things. They told him how helpful it can be to talk to someone who really gets it.

The whole event was a godsend. Ashton was a godsend. If it hadn't been for Ashton and for SRT Prosthetics, Marty would have never fully made peace with his decision. But as he looked at all of these amputees living normal lives, exercising, helping others, he knew that he had made the right decision.

He was ready.

Chapter 24

The day had finally arrived. Jess, his parents, Ryan, Hayley, and Joe went to the hospital with Marty for the amputation. As they rode down to Indy, Marty focused in on the pain in his foot. He realized that this would be the last time he would feel that pain, the last time he would feel anything at all in that foot. What would it be like to not feel it anymore?

He had spent part of the night before just staring at his leg. The whole thing seemed surreal. That night he went to bed with his leg in tact, and the next night he would go to bed without it. He thought about his conversations with Ashton and the other people at the event. The memories of their words of encouragement kept the darkness at bay that morning.

The car ride went by quickly and with minimal conversation. The atmosphere was somewhere between awkward and tense. Nobody really knew what to say to Marty, and that was just fine. He preferred that nobody said anything. He was just ready to get it over with. He was ready to be done thinking about it.

When they arrived, they saw the workers compensation lady waiting for them. She, of course, had to be at every single appointment, surgeries included. She didn't say much today though, just a simple hello before taking a seat in the waiting area. Marty wasn't sure exactly what she'd be taking notes on that day.

The leg's officially gone now. So, yeah.

Jess did most of the talking as the registrar checked him in for the procedure. He wasn't necessarily nervous, just chomping at the bit. The registration felt like it took half a century. They sat in the waiting room for about ten minutes before a nurse called him back for his pre-op vitals. He hugged his kids and told him he loved them before he and Jess walked back into the surgery department.

Jess held his hand as they followed the nurse to a small room. Marty sat in the chair and answered the nurse's pre-op questions as she took his blood pressure and measured his oxygen. His blood pressure was a little high.

"That's normal before a surgery," she assured him. "It's still within normal limits for this kind of procedure."

He nodded his head. When she was finished, she told them the doctor would be in to see him shortly and left the room.

"You good, babe?" Jess asked.

"Yeah," he answered. "Ready to get this show on the road."

They didn't have to wait long before the doctor came in.

"Hi there. Long time, no see," the doctor said. "You ready?"

"Ready as I'll ever be," Marty replied.

"Any questions before we get you all prepped and ready for surgery?"

Marty shook his head.

"Nope. Let's do it."

The doctor left the room and sent the nurse back in to get them. When they reached the doors that went to the surgical area, it was time to say goodbye to Jess. He wrapped her up in his arms and held her tight. And as he kissed her, he felt a little bit of his worry melt away.

"I love you," she whispered. "It's all gonna be okay."

"I love you, too."

And with that, he followed the nurse through the locked doors. They had him get into a gown, and the anesthesiologist wasted no time in getting started. As Marty stared up at the fluorescent lights, he couldn't help but wish that he were looking at the stars instead. And before he knew it, everything faded to darkness.

***

When Marty woke up from surgery, the first thing he saw was Jess. She smiled at him, and for a moment he forgot where he was and what was going on. It wasn't until he felt a strange imbalance, until he tried to move his left foot that he remembered.

He slowly lifted his head up and looked down. And that's when he saw it. Or, rather, that's when he saw what was missing. And in that moment, for the first time in months, he broke down.

He didn't think he would lose it like this. He had expected to be upset, but not like this. The tears flowed down his cheeks as his wife hugged him.

He felt the worries overwhelm him even more than they had before he met with Ashton.

He was crippled.

He was disabled.

He would be a burden to his family.

He wouldn't be able to work.

These thoughts, these lies overwhelmed his mind and plagued his soul in those first moments of waking. He sobbed into Jess' shoulder as she tried to console him.

He was thankful that Jess was the only one in the room. He didn't want his children to see him like this. What if his mom saw him like this? She would lose it, too.

"Don't let anyone else come in yet," he whispered to his wife.

"I won't, babe," she promised. "I won't. It's okay. It's gonna be fine."

He cried for a while longer, but he eventually pulled himself together. He thought again of Ashton and of all the other amputees he had met in Muncie that day. They lived normal lives, fulfilling lives. Their amputations didn't destroy them, and their prosthetics enabled them to accomplish all they wanted to and more.

He meditated on these thoughts as he let go of Jess and leaned back in the bed. These had to be his thoughts from now on. The positives had to rule; he wouldn't allow the darkness to sit on the throne of his mind ever again.

"I'm okay now," he told Jess. "I'm okay. You can send them in."

She nodded her head and walked out into the hallway. She returned with Joe, his mom, and his dad.

"Hey," Joe said as he entered the room.

"Hey," Marty replied.

Joe walked over to his bed and looked at what was remaining of Marty's left leg. The sutures went across the base of the leg and up the sides. Joe let out a chuckle.

"It looks like a catfish," he mumbled.

"Joe Garrett!" his mother exclaimed as she slapped his arm.

But Marty and Jess just laughed. Marty looked down at it and smirked.

"Huh, he's right. It kind of does."

Everyone was laughing at this point, even Irene. And as Marty looked around at all the smiling faces, he realized that Ashton had been right. Things were going to be okay. And the doctor was right, as well. This was the next logical step. And Marty's anxiety about his next steps? Well, that was an unfounded worry.

He didn't have to worry about his next steps so long as his family was walking next to him. And they would be. Always.

Chapter 25

For two and a half months, Marty recovered from his amputation and got used to his prosthetic leg. It was easier than he thought it would be, truthfully. He had become so used to painful surgeries that, in the end, only brought him more pain. Now here he was post surgery able to run, play with his nieces, and go through his daily routine with no pain.

It took a long time for it to seem real. He had forgotten what it felt like to live without constant pain. It got to a point that one day when he got a headache, he realized that before the amputation, he wouldn't have even been bothered by it because the pain in his foot would have completely overshadowed it. Funny how a headache can bring about such a revelation.

On a sunny but cold December morning, Marty was driving himself and Jess to his appointment with his orthopedic surgeon. There was no ice or snow on the roads, so the trip was quick. This time last year, he was starting desk duty in immense pain. Now he was on his way to what he hoped would be his final appointment before he would be cleared for full duty.

They pulled into the parking lot at the same time as the workers compensation woman. She got out of the car and smiled at them.

"Well, this may be the last time we get to go to an appointment together," she said.

"Hopefully," Marty replied. "Don't take it personally, though. We're just ready to get things back to normal."

She laughed.

"I understand completely," she said.

The three of them walked into the office. Marty checked himself in and then took a seat next to his wife. The two looked at each other and smiled from ear to ear.

"This is it," she whispered.

Marty thought about how far he had come in a year and a half. He had gone from nearly bleeding out on the street to barely being able to walk to now being pain free and able to go about his daily life with little to no difficulty. Sure, having to put his leg on in the morning wasn't exactly ideal, but he was thankful that he had a leg to put on. He was thankful that his life was getting back to normal. Well, to a new normal, anyway.

"Marty?"

The medical assistant waved to them from the doorway, and the three of them followed her back to the exam room. She told him that since he had worn basketball shorts, he wouldn't need to get into a gown. Though, she expressed surprise at his clothing choice considering it was near freezing outside.

"Well I mean, only one of my legs could potentially get frostbite," he informed her.

She chuckled as she took his vitals. The doctor entered the room just as she was finishing up her documenting.

"Well, how are we feeling?" he asked.

"Great. Better than ever," Marty replied.

"Excellent. Let's take a look."

Marty took off the prosthetic so the doctor could examine things.

"Everything looks great," he affirmed. "Ready to get back into the field?"

"More than ready!" Marty exclaimed.

"Well, let's get you back out there then. I want you to follow up with me in six months, but I'm going to clear you to go back to full duty. I'll go put together the paperwork, and the medical assistant will be back in with you shortly."

"Thank you," Marty said.

"Yes, thank you so much," Jess echoed.

About five minutes later, the medical assistant returned with the paperwork. Marty's precious ticket back into the field, back into the K9 Unit. He could have kissed that paperwork!

The three of them walked back into the waiting room.

"Congratulations on all your hard work," the workers compensation woman said. "It's been a long journey. You should be very proud of yourself."

"Thank you," Marty replied.

"I just have a quick paper for you to sign before we say goodbye," she added as she pulled a paper from her folder.

She placed it on a clipboard and handed it to him with a pen. Marty cast her a confused look as Jess examined the paperwork from behind him.

"What's this?" he asked.

"It's your paperwork discharging us from further liability," she said. "Now that you're back to full duty, we're no longer responsible for your care."

Marty practically let the clipboard slip from his hands, and his jaw dropped open. He looked to Jess. Her jaw had done the same.

"What do you mean you're no longer responsible?" Jess asked. "Who's responsible?"

"Look, this is going to be a lifelong expense for me. These outer covers for the prosthetic are four hundred bucks and I have to replace them three times a month. I have to get a whole new prosthetic twice a year. I mean, we're talking hundreds of thousands of dollars over the course of my lifetime."

"I understand it's a big expense. I'm just letting you know that my company aren't the ones who are responsible for it. I'm sorry," she explained.

"Look, I get that you're just trying to do your job. I respect that. But I'm not signing anything until I figure out who's paying for this," Marty replied as he held the clipboard out to her.

The woman stared at him in shock, but she took the clipboard back.

"I understand," she said. "You'll need to reach out to your human resources department to get this figured out, though, because this form will have to be signed eventually."

Marty looked to his wife. He could see the anger burning in her eyes, and he decided that the sooner they could get out of there, the better.

"I understand. Thank you," he said as he grabbed Jess' hand.

The two of them quickly walked to their car, and the moment the doors shut, Jess lost it.

"What the hell does she mean they're not paying for it? Who's paying for it?"

"I don't know, Jess. We'll figure it out."

She was panicking, and it was understandable. They were talking about hundreds of thousands of dollars. He grabbed her hand.

"Look at all the shit we've gotten through already, babe. We'll get through this. We'll figure it out."

He could feel some of the tension release from her body, but not all of it. She was still angry. He was angry, too, but he was trying to keep it together. He would call the City human resources department as soon as he got home.

Somebody was going to take responsibility for these bills, and it wasn't going to be him.

Chapter 26

"We'll get back to you."

That was the answer that Marty had gotten from the human resources department. After he had waited a sufficient amount of time without hearing anything, he called them again. Well, according to the City, the workers compensation company was responsible for the cost of his lifelong care. But wait, according to the workers compensation company, the City was responsible for the cost of his lifelong care.

And that was it. They were at a standstill. Neither party would agree to cover Marty's lifelong care, and he couldn't do anything about it. He couldn't go back to work until it got sorted. And he would need another cover for his prosthetic in a matter of days.

And nobody would pay for it.

Word of the battle spread throughout the city building. This person told this person who told that person until a majority of the working people in downtown Anderson knew about the battle. That was how Marty got the phone call that would change his fortune.

The woman who called him was Lisa DeLey, an attorney who worked in downtown Anderson. She told him that she had heard about his situation through the grapevine and that she wanted to help him, pro bono. It wouldn't take her too long to find the answer to the great question and get some results for him.

He couldn't believe what he was hearing. Pro bono. The news brought Jess to tears, and Marty must have thanked her at least a dozen times. She told him that after all he and his family had sacrificed, he deserved to have this situation resolved.

DeLey split the work with another attorney, Mark Dudley, and within two weeks, they had put together the proper paperwork and sent it to the City. After much research, they had determined that it was within the City's contract with the workers compensation company that any expenses associated with lifelong illness or injury were the responsibility of the City. Once the facts had been presented to the City, it was impossible for them to deny what Marty was owed. They agreed, in writing, to cover all expenses relating to Marty's leg for the remainder of his life. And, after this agreement was given the seal of approval by DeLey and Dudley, Marty signed the worker compensation woman's paper.

It was a frustrating situation, to say the least. Things should have been smooth sailing after Marty got the "ok" to go back to full duy. He shouldn't have had to receive legal counsel to get someone to pay for his expenses. After all, he nearly gave his life serving and protecting.

He tried to remember that nobody was being malicious. It wasn't that they didn't think he *deserved* to have his medical needs paid for; each person was just trying to protect the business they served. That's just business; Marty understood that. The only thing he wished was that somebody had known what needed to be done and done it. The waiting, the uncertainty, it was a lot to deal with, too much for a family adjusting to a whole new normal.

But, he was thankful for DeLey and Dudley. They spent hours of their free time working on this for him, and he hadn't even asked them to. They just did it out of the kindness of their hearts. Without them, who knows what would have happened? The whole situation only strengthened his faith. God had made it a habit of sending him exactly who he needed exactly when he needed them.

He thought about this as he lay in bed the night before he went back to full duty. Though the past year and a half had been full of trials and tribulations, it had also been full of miracles.

Miracles that changed his life for the better.

Miracles that had proved to him that he was stronger than he ever imagined.

Miracles that made him a better father, a better son, a better husband, and a better police officer.

And before he drifted off to sleep, he thanked God for every single one of them.

Chapter 27

Each day that he works, Marty is amazed at how much easier life is with a prosthetic than with a painful, floppy, enormous foot. In truth, he functions just as well as he did before the shooting! Ashton had been right all along. And to think he assumed the kid was just trying to make a quick sale!

Marty has a new partner now. Rico is a German shepherd, and he was admittedly much easier to train than Kilo. But Marty thinks of Kilo every single day. There will always be a hole in his heart that cannot be filled by another dog, by anything or anyone on Earth. Each day that he gets ready for work, he remembers Kilo, because without his loyal partner, he wouldn't be able to go to work. He wouldn't be able to see his kids grow up or grow old with the love of his life. So each day as he thanks God for another day of life, he also thanks God for Kilo.

Marty will never be able to go too long without thinking about the shooting. Each day when he wakes up and has to put his prosthetic on before he can start his day, he is forced to remember all the damage that the shooter caused. But each time he has to do this, he is thankful that this injury happened to him and not to someone else. He is thankful that Williams and Guthrie and Bailey all made it out of there safely, and he is thankful that no other officers were gravely injured that night.

Each time he puts his prosthetic on, he also thinks of Mr. Shull whose life was so cruelly taken away. He talks to Mrs. Shull every now and then; she's a very kind lady. He wishes that he could have saved her husband, that the two of them could've grown old together.

Sometimes it all overwhelms him, but it doesn't last long. Because the moment he sees his wife, the moment he hears one of his children call out for him in the morning, he knows that that shooter didn't destroy him. He took a lot, but he didn't take everything.

So he stands onto his foot and his prosthetic, and he smiles at the day. Every day.

He thanks God for his family. He thanks God for his health. He thanks God for the opportunity to serve and protect. And he thanks God for the Warrior Mindset that he gave to Joe, that he passed on to Marty, and that now is his motto. That now is his family's motto.

Born to die... Just not today.

Epilogue

Joe and Marty have made an impact on thousands of lives not only through their heroic actions, but through telling their stories. In 2015, Brad Smith from the magazine *K9 Cop* reached out to Marty for an interview. This 2 ½ hour long phone call led to an article in the magazine, which led to a call from Jeff Barrett, a K9 officer from Florida. Barrett puts on a seminar called HITS (Handler Instruction and Training Seminar) where K9 handlers from all over the country come to hear stories and learn new skills. He invited Marty and Joe to attend and tell their story at the seminar in 2015.

The brothers went from one seminar in 2015 to attending 8-12 speaking events a year in the following years. They have spoken at events from local departments all the way up to events for the US Department of Justice. In June of 2017, the brothers even got invited to be a part of a podcast for *Barstool Heartland*. Both also still serve full time on the Anderson Police Department.

Marty and Jess now have three children together: Marlie, Jax, and a newborn son, Hayes. Ryan is attending trade school in Texas, and Hayley is working at St. Vincent Anderson as a patient access representative while she works on her nursing degree.

Sophie is now a freshman and Ava is now a seventh-grader. Joe and Mendy also have a five-year-old foster son, Keighton, whose adoption they expect to be finalized by the end of 2018. Kegan is working as an IT professional, and Cara is working at a doctor's office and is now happily married to Officer Joe Todd of the Anderson Police Department. The couple have an infant son named Hank.

The family is closer now than they have ever been, and each day brings them closer to each other and to God. It is a dark, scary world out there for law enforcement, and it's even scarier for their families. But the Dulworths and the Garretts make the decision each day to place their faith in God. And each day, they face the world with a smirk on their faces and say, "Not today!"

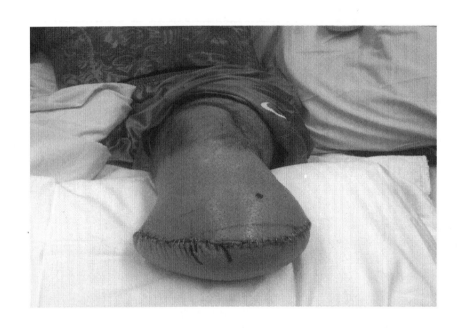

The Catfish

Marty doesn't let his prosthetic slow him down. He is living his best life, and he never takes anything for granted.

Afterword

When Joe Garrett first sent me a text that said, "Hey. You write books, right?", I had no idea what I was about to get myself into. I hadn't spoken to him since I left my patient access job at St Vincent Anderson ER. He presented this book idea to me, and I could hardly believe that he was offering me the job. A nonfiction project for two badass police officers? Count me in!

As I conducted my interviews to put this book together, I learned a lot about Joe Garrett, more than I had ever learned at the hospital. And, of course, I got to meet his brother, Marty, and the rest of their close-knit family. As much as I learned about the night of the shooting and the events that played out afterward, I learned even more about what law enforcement families go through on a daily basis.

Our current political climate is one wherein speaking and writing about law enforcement is tricky. I don't need to point to any particular instances to make my point; we all know. But, regardless of anyone's opinion on these events and this tumultuous period of time in our nation's history, I believe that we can all agree on one thing: law enforcement families are struggling.

Try to imagine that each day you say goodbye to your spouse or parent or sibling, you have no idea whether or not they will be coming home after their shift. And although you know that this is a possibility, you can't dwell on it. And although you can't dwell on it, you have to somehow always ensure that you are prepared for it if it happens. It's a balancing act, one that few people outside of law enforcement families can manage.

This project has been an incredible learning experience for me. Not only have I gotten to know an amazing family and put their story into book form, but I've also been given the opportunity to see things from a different perspective. It has given me the chance to practice sympathy and compassion and understanding.

Thank you, Joe and Marty, for trusting me with this project. I can only hope that I've done your story justice.

-Sydney M. Hunt

Made in the USA
Columbia, SC
28 September 2018